Ask Dr. Mike:
Frequently Asked
Questions
About Psychology

Michael Atkinson
University of Western Ontario

MCGRAW-HILL RYERSON LIMITED

Toronto   Montréal   Boston   Burr Ridge, IL   Dubuque, IA
Madison, WI   New York   San Francisco
St. Louis   Bangkok   Bogotá   Caracas   Kuala Lumpur   Lisbon
London   Madrid   Mexico City   Milan
New Delhi   Santiago   Seoul   Singapore   Sydney   Taipei

Ask Dr. Mike:
Frequently Asked Questions About Psychology
by Michael Atkinson

Custom Publisher: Jeff Snook
Senior Custom Reprint Coordinator: Betty Tustin
Cover Design: Rebecca Walker

ISBN: 0-07-074625-7

Printed and bound in Canada

Dedication

To all those psychology students who have asked such wonderful questions over the years.

There are no "stupid" questions, only inadequate answers.

Acknowledgments

Rarely is it the case that a book comes together without the author receiving a great deal of help and support. This one is no exception. Thanks to the great production staff at McGraw Hill Ryerson—you are all amazing, especially with my "just in time" schedule. Special thanks to Jeff Snook who insisted (on many occasions) that I do this book for McGraw.

Over the years, there have been many people at MHR who have encouraged me to author Canadian texts and have supported me in this venture. Some of these folks are still with MHR while others have left McGraw for other ventures. Thanks to Ralph Courtney, Petra Cooper, Peter McCullough, Joe Saundercook, Veronica Visentin, Margaret Henderson, James Buchanan, Sharon Loeb, Patrick Ferrier, Darren Hick, Suzanne Simpson Millar, John Dill, Tim McCleary, Karen Ritcey, & Joanna Cotton. Finally, a very special thanks to my friend and publishing confidante, Marcie Mealia. Marcie, it was your spark that ignited many psychology authors and gave us the confidence to pursue projects we had always wanted to do.

 # Table of Contents

1 Ask Dr. Mike

Introduction

Welcome to Ask Dr. Mike! Below you will find my rationale for this book along with some suggestions for both students and instructors. So please enjoy and never stop asking questions.

Questions, questions, questions. Almost every student has at least one question about introductory psychology that they really would like to have answered. How does the brain work? Is there any difference between the brain and the mind? Why do we dream? What makes people like or hate one another? Why do some people go "crazy" while others remain "normal"?

For the past 24 years, I have been teaching Introductory Psychology at the University of Western Ontario in London, Ontario, Canada. I have taught courses at a variety of levels ranging from first year to senior graduate classes, but I find the introductory course the most challenging. The reason involves the type of question that students will ask. Whenever an issue arises, senior undergraduates and graduate students will tend to focus on methodology or the details of some psychological theory. This is fine--it is what we train students to do. But first year students will take a different approach. They will ask you a broader question, one that we often forget about as instructors: "Why would anyone want to know that?"

This can be quite perplexing to the instructor. After all, we *all know* why it is necessary to study the anatomical details of the human eye. Or the importance of cognitive dissonance theory as the groundwork for attitude change. Or why you have to learn statistics in order to understand psychology. I agree. But the trick is not in the knowing, it is in the ability to explain the usefulness of concepts to others.

I've had the pleasure of trying to explain concepts to students both in class at Western and online at various websites. Many of the questions in this book come from these sources.

About the questions in this book. Over the years, there are thousands of questions that students have asked about psychology. For this book I have selected those that were asked most frequently, or those that dealt with an interesting or complicated topic. Frequent questions reflect the requirements for a degree or career in psychology, explanations of how a particular drug works, and just about anything to do with dreams. The more complicated topics tend to be statistics, neurons, sensory systems, conditioning, and understanding the role of theory in scientific investigation. On the more interesting side, we have some "folklore" questions ("Are carrots really good for your eyesight?"), some calendar questions ("Is there a chemical in turkey that makes you sleepy?"), and some "I've always wondered..." questions ("If you remove a large portion of someone's brain, do you have to fill the space with anything to retain balance?").

The chapters in this book are somewhat arbitrary. I have used chapter headings similar to those found in most introductory text books, but the questions were not necessarily asked during the coverage of that chapter. For example, a question on drug action ("How does Ecstasy work") may arise in the biopsychology chapter, the consciousness chapter, or when we begin to discuss psychological treatment. It may come up after a particular story runs in the national media. So even though the ecstasy question is answered in the biopsychology chapter, it is relevant for other topics as well. Similarly, you will find questions about dreams in Chapter 5 (Consciousness and Motivation) as well as Chapter 9 (Personality). Those in Chapter 5 are more directly related to sleep, while those in Chapter 9 deal more with a Freudian interpretation of dreams.

Note: In answering these questions, I have tried to be as accurate as possible and address the question from the point of view of the introductory psychology student. In many cases, the answer is a good deal more complicated than I have suggested. So please do not take these answers as the definitive statement on a particular topic. In addition, any issue of a medical or professional nature (e.g., a sleep disorder, psychological problem) should be referred to an appropriate mental or physical health professional. My answer is intended as background material only.

Some suggestions on how to use this book. Questions and answers can be fun to read, but I invite you also to think critically about each of the items in this book. As you read a question, try to come up with a brief answer on your own. Jot down a few key points. Think about where this question would fit in your own text book. What are the relevant terms and concepts one might need to know in order to answer this question? Is this an important question? Why? What other concepts might the answer be related to? How does this issue relate to your own life? After you compare your answer to mine, think about those points you might have missed. Are they important? Think about the points I might have missed. Should I have included those in my own answer?

A note for instructors. To help integrate this book into your course, you might ask your students to choose a question from each chapter and perform the critical thinking exercise outlined above. Students could submit a short one-page "essay" on that question along with another question that they think would be important to ask about this topic.

You can also use some of the questions as lecture starters--points for discussion prior to the beginning of a topic. This can work very well by using a method similar to brain-storming. Choose a particular topic or question (e.g., "How does ecstasy work?") and begin the class by asking, "What have you heard about the drug, ecstasy? What have you read about it, or what have you seen on T.V.?" This method will allow students to voice an opinion in a very low-pressure format. You are not asking for a description of the physiological mechanism, nor does anyone have to identify themselves as an ecstasy user--you're merely asking what people have heard about ecstasy. As students tell you what they've heard, write the points on the blackboard or overhead. After a few minutes, you will have a number of topics and issues to explore. In using this method, it is important to not leave students with false impressions. For example, if someone has heard that ecstasy is "relatively harmless", it would be important to point out the potential hazards.

Got a question about introductory psychology? If you have a question and would like to send it to me, please feel free to do so. You can reach me at

atkinson@uwo.ca

I look forward to hearing from you.

answers) are posted every month. Note: we try to answer all questions (at least privately) within a reasonable time frame.

Learning Activities. This feature presents a number of online interactive demonstrations and tutorials on topics ranging from the functioning of neurons to sex differences in depression. Many of these activities require critical thinking skills, actual experimental data collection, and active web searches. The activities are both fun and informative and take about an average of 15 to 20 minutes to complete.

Op Ed Forum. Each month a guest contributor will post an original essay on some topic of relevance to psychology. Many contributors are faculty members, but there are also a number of student essays in this section. *The Psychology Place*™ conducts a student Op Ed Forum contest with a cash prize for the winning entry. That student's essay is published in our forum section. Note: Readers are invited to join an online discussion about the essay with the author and colleagues.

Research News. Twice a month a new article is posted that provides a summary of topical research. The author outlines the pro and con positions on the topic and provides a number of print and Web references for further research. This is a great place for students to begin a literature search for research projects.

Teaching Resources. This feature is provided for as a resource to instructors who are looking for demonstrations to use in the classroom, or for ways to integrate *The Psychology Place*™ into their own teaching. There are numerous examples and tips available.

Best of the Web. More than a listing of favorite links, the best web sites are examined, annotated and checked for accuracy. New sites are added every month and you can search the data base using psychological terms and topics.

Test Flight. If *The Psychology Place*™ came packaged with your text book, it is likely that practice exams for your book are available here. Test Flight allows you to choose the chapters you want to be examined on and the number of questions you want to try. Your practice exam is graded automatically, and if you got the item wrong, the correct answer will be indicated. This is one of the most popular areas of *The Psychology Place*™. Note: you can select a general test is your textbook is not listed on the site.

Scientific American. This section provides articles online from Scientific American. The articles have been selected based on their relevance for psychology and include links to the glossary and other web resources.

Glossary. *The Psychology Place*™ Glossary contains over 1000 terms and is accessible from virtually anywhere on the site. Many of the entries include sound files illustrating the correct pronunciation.

In addition to these standard features, you'll find new ones introduced on a regular basis such as the Psychology Crossword and Quote of the Day. *The Psychology Place*™ is a valuable resource for both students and faculty in psychology.

Got a question about introductory psychology? If you have a question and would like to send it to me, please feel free to do so. You can reach me at

atkinson@julian.uwo.ca

Or visit us at *The Psychology Place*™. I look forward to hearing from you.

General Issues, History & Methods

What's really important to study in a psychology text? Do I have to know the names and dates? Why do we bother studying statistics? These are questions that I get all the time both in class and on the Psychology Place website. The answers will vary from instructor to instructor, but I think that we all want our students to understand what psychologists do and to gain an appreciation for theory and theory testing. This means understanding the scientific method, knowing how to construct an experiment, and being able to use statistics to interpret data. The history of Psychology is perhaps a little easier to capture as compared to other scientific disciplines--we've only been around for about 100 years!

Q: **My textbook seems to have a LOT of information. How do I know what's important (1)?**

A: This is a question that I encounter often and one that is always difficult to answer. First, let me say that the best answer to this question will come from your own instructor. Only she or he knows exactly what will be emphasized and tested on. But having said that, there are a few general guidelines I can offer. Theories and concepts are more important than facts and individual experiments. If you understand a theory, you will be able to predict what the results of an experiment (the "facts") should be. Experiments themselves are important to the extent that they support or fail to support a theory. In general, names and dates are not that important. The exceptions are in the introductory chapter of your text (where you probably will be expected to know the names of people) and the really big figures in psychology such as Freud, Piaget, and Skinner (the big names usually have an approach or theory named after them). Check the study guide for your textbook. It will help you to determine what is and is not important in each chapter.

Q: **In order to go to graduate school in psychology, do I need to get a B.A. or a B.S. (2)?**

A: In almost all cases, it does not matter. Admission to graduate school is based more on your marks, your scores on aptitude tests (such as the GRE), and your letters of reference. Whether you receive a B.A. or B.S. (a B.Sc. in Canada) often depends on where psychology is placed in at your undergraduate institution (e.g., Arts, Science, etc.). At the University of Western Ontario, psychology is in the Faculty of Social Science. The typical degree is a B.A.

There are a few graduate programs where it might matter whether your degree is a B.A. or B.S. For example, programs in neuroscience will typically "require" a B.S. The requirement really reflects the courses you need to take (e.g., science courses such as chemistry, math, etc.) more than the degree itself. You should check with graduate departments that you are interested in and see what the exact requirements are for their program.

Q: **Do I need to go to medical school for a career in research psychology (3)?**

A: Glad to hear that you're interested in pursuing psychological research! You do not need to go to medical school to become a research psychologist. You would only go in this direction if your goal were to become a psychiatrist rather than a psychologist (psychiatrists hold an M.D. degree). To do research, you will need a Ph.D. in psychology. You should first complete your undergraduate degree in psychology, then go on to graduate school and concentrate on a specific area or field of psychology, such as clinical, developmental, or social psychology.

As an undergraduate, you should select courses related to the specialty that interests you along with courses on research and methodology. Every school is different, but most will require a course in research methods and perhaps a separate course in statistics. There may be other program requirements. For example, my department at the University of Western Ontario requires a course in methods, statistics, math, and two specific research methodology courses in a particular content area. You should check with the academic counselor in your department about course selection.

Q: **I am interested in becoming a psychiatrist and I am wondering about what it takes to accomplish that? Like what are the best schools to go to and how long of an education process it is, how many more years of school do I have left after I finish college? Also what else could I do in order to distinguish myself from other potential**

medical school applicants to increase my chances of getting into medical school (4)?

A: As you indicate, the road to becoming a psychiatrist involves going to medical school, so the first thing you need to consider is the requirements for med school. Most medical programs will require some kind of "pre-med" degree...a science degree with specific courses such as biology, organic chemistry, etc. You need to check with the med school you are interested in for specific program requirements. The program you are interested in may or may not allow for early acceptance (i.e., acceptance after 2nd year without finishing a degree), but most programs will ask for a least a 3 year degree. Once you are admitted to medical school, the program typically is 3 years (this will vary from place to place), and this would be followed by a one year internship. At this point, you would be an M.D., but to become a psychiatrist, you would have to specialize further. As a resident, you would take specific training in psychiatry, and the program could be up an additional 4 years. So, if we add it all up: 3 year college/university degree + 3 year M.D. degree, + internship + resident = about 11 years total to reach your goal. For comparison, it would take about the same amount of time to complete a degree in clinical psychology (typically 4 year undergraduate degree + 5 or 6 years in graduate school).

Entrance to medical school is extremely competitive and to be seriously considered, students need to have an average in the 86% - 92% range (this, of course will vary from place to place). Thus, the number one consideration for a student is good academic performance. However, grades are not the only consideration at most schools. Other factors include volunteer work in the community, letters of reference from various community sources, etc. So once again, you need to check with the programs you are interested in to see exactly what criteria are involved in their admission decisions. Most schools have information listed on their web sites, so that's probably a good place to start. Good luck!

Q: **I read in one question that being a psychiatrist requires medical school. Does being a therapist require that also (5)?**

A: Medical school is a requirement for psychiatry only. The reason is that a psychiatrist can prescribe drugs and you must be an M.D. to do this. A therapist may be a psychiatrist, a psychologist, or someone trained in a particular method or style of therapy (e.g., a marriage therapist; a Jungian therapist, etc.). In most states and provinces, the term "therapist" is not protected by law— anyone can call him or herself a therapist. This is one of the reasons to be very careful when choosing a therapist. You may not be getting the high-quality psychological service you think you're getting. The best way to find out is to check with the state or provincial registration authority (e.g., the American Psychological Association), or simply ask your family doctor.

Q: **What kind of grades do you need in high school to be a psychologist and what classes should you take (6)?**

A: Your high school grades will not necessarily reflect your ability to become a psychologist, but they are critical for getting into the college or university of your choice. The admission average will vary from place to place (at my university you must have a minimum average of 78% in your last 6 high school courses). Therefore, always strive to do your best. At university, it is wise to try to maintain an "A" average in order to make yourself an attractive candidate for graduate school.

What classes should you take? Once again, the requirements will vary from place to place, but I believe that it is useful to have a background in Biology, Math, and English. Any course that encourages critical thinking also is valuable.

Q: **Where did psychology first appear and in what year (7)?**

A: The answer really depends on what you define as "psychology". There were many individuals working in psychology-related areas in the first half of the nineteenth century (and even before that). Most of this work was on physiology (e.g., Sir Charles Bell and Johannes Muller). Fechner outlined his ideas about psychophysics in the middle part of the century. However, most people credit Wilhelm Wundt with the founding of modern psychology. E.G. Boring notes in his history of psychology that Wundt is the first person who could properly be called a psychologist, and his establishment of the first psychological laboratory at Leipzig in 1879 is taken as the birth of modern experimental psychology. Others have claimed that William James was the first to establish a lab in 1877 at Harvard, but Boring notes that this was a more informal lab and that, in fact, Wundt had similar facilities as early as 1875.

Q: **Who is the most "famous" psychologist (8)?**

A: It really depends on how you define "fame." Many people suggest we look for evidence of one's impact on the entire field of psychology. One way to judge this is to see how often an individual is cited or referenced in the works of others. There is an easy way to check this. Many libraries carry a citation index in their reference section (there is a separate citation index for science and for social science). It is published every six months and covers a wide variety of journals in the field. All you have to do is look up a particular author and the index will list any article published in the last six months in which that author was referenced. By this measure, the individual who has been referenced more than anyone else is exactly who you might expect—Sigmund Freud.

Q: **Why does psychology favor Darwin's theory of evolution over creationism (9)?**

A: Let me start by noting that psychology does not really "favor" one theory over another. Certain theories complement our definition of psychology— the science of mental processes and behavior— while others do not. In this context, Darwin's theory of evolution follows the rules for theory-building in the science of psychology, while creationism does not follow these rules. Note that creationism may meet the standards outlined by another discipline where Darwin may fall short. We can only judge a theory within the constraints of a particular field of study.

So what counts as theory in psychology? Psychology is a behavioral science, and as such, follows the rules of the scientific method. Within this context, one of the most important rules is that theories must be testable. Good theories make clear predictions—predictions that when tested can either offer support for the theory or fail to support it. A theory cannot simultaneously take the presence and the absence of an effect as supportive. It must be precise. Using this standard, Darwin's theory is more testable than creationism. Thus, we "favor" this theory because it follows the scientific method more closely than does creationism.

Q: **Why do people talk about Freud so much—he seems like a bit of a "wacko" to me (10)?**

A: While some of Freud's ideas seem "odd" to us today, we need to remember where he was coming from. As a medical doctor at the turn of the twentieth century, Freud was trying to understand and treat what appeared to be real problems that had no physical basis. He was influenced strongly by the theories and practices of Charcot--a French academic who treated a disorder known as hysteria with the use of hypnosis (and sometimes, an early version of electroshock therapy). As a clinician, Freud built his theories on his own observations of his patients and how they seemed to respond to various treatments. Freud's approach to personality was not always accepted, even by his own students. Karl Jung, for example, broke ranks with Freud because he felt that Freud placed far too much emphasis on sexual development.

Why do we still talk about Freud? The ideas of Sigmund Freud seem to have found there way into issues ranging from psychology to art, from literature to philosophy, and so on. Something about what he had to say seems to touch a wide variety of interests. Perhaps the reason is that Freud gave us the notion of the unconscious and made us consider that there is a "dark" side to human existence, one that we might never really know about because it is out of our awareness.

Q: **Who was right—Freud or Jung (11)?**

A: Whenever we get into a comparison of theories, we don't really talk about which one is "right" and which is "wrong". Theories are not so much right or wrong—they are more or less useful. A useful theory will explain many different sets of facts and will be supported by the data. Less useful theories are difficult to test, and may not have much research support.

So who is more useful—Freud or Jung? This is a difficult question. Both deal with concepts that are hard to test (e.g., the unconscious), and at the same time, both are very broad in their explanation of many areas of human behavior. Both theories discuss the notion of resolving conflicts. For Freud these conflicts are sexual in nature, but for Jung they are not. In the end, Freud has probably had more impact than Jung (although many will disagree).

Q: **What is a "placebo" (12)?**

A: A placebo is an inactive and harmless substance that may have an effect on patients or research subjects, because it is administered just as an active agent is, and therefore the subjects believe it is affecting them.

Sometimes if you expect that a particular drug will cure or relieve your ailments, that belief may itself reduce or eliminate the symptoms. This response is called "the placebo effect." When testing new drugs, one group of participants will receive the active drug, while a second group will receive the identical instructions, packaging, and procedure, but the pills or "placebo" will have no active ingredient. Therefore, scientists can be certain that any effects are due to the drug alone.

We must protect against placebo effects when doing research. For example, I may be interested in a new study method and assign one group of students to use the new method and a second group to use the old method. If I find that the experimental group does better on an exam, how can I be sure that it was due to my new study method? Perhaps the students in this group are merely responding to special treatment. I need to run a placebo group here as well, one that receives attention, but does not include the active ingredient—my new study method.

Q: **What's the difference between a random sample and random assignment (13)?**

A: Students often confuse the meanings of these two methods in experimental design. Both methods strive to reduce bias in a research study. But the procedure used in each method is quite different. Whenever we conduct a study, we must have some means of choosing the group of people for the investigation. For example, if I am interested in the responses of college students to stress, I might ask every single college student in North America to describe how they respond to stressful situations. While this seems like a good idea, it is not very practical—it would cost a fortune and I probably could not get every single student to participate.

So I have to limit my investigation. For this reason, psychologists often conduct studies using a small group of first-year psychology students. In order to make sure that the studies' results apply to the larger group (i.e., the findings generalize to the larger group), they choose the people for their study at random. For example, you could pick names or numbers out of a hat or use a table of random numbers. There are other ways to insure generalizability, but random sampling is one of the most frequently used methods.

Random assignment refers to the allocation of

research participants to groups. For example, I might be interested in the effects of a new drug on memory. The experimental group receives the drug while the control group receives a placebo. As subjects show up to the lab, I should assign them to either the experimental group or the control group on a random basis. If I use another procedure (e.g., experimental group in the morning and control group in the afternoon), I would introduce a confound into the study. I would not be able to tell if any results were due to the drug or to differences in people's performance in the morning versus the afternoon.

Q: **I'm confused about independent and dependent variables. Can you help (14)?**

A: The concept of independent and dependent variables in experimental design is difficult for many students. I find that the easiest way to keep these variables straight is to remember that the independent variable is the one the experimenter manipulates. It is the treatment (for example, drug level) or situation (a weight loss program) that changes from one condition to another. The dependent variable is the one that is measured or recorded. It is the same for all participants.

For example, let's say that I'm interested in the effects of caffeine on learning. One group of subjects drinks five cups of coffee while reading chapter 2 from their text. A second group drinks two cups of coffee while reading, and a third group drinks no coffee at all. When they are finished, all subjects take a test based on the material in chapter 2. In this example, the independent variable is the amount of coffee consumed (five, two or no cups). The dependent variable (the one that is measured and is the same for all participants) is the score achieved on the test. Note that I would certainly expect each participant's score to be different on the test, but every person is given exactly the same test. If we were conducting this study, we would probably want to add at least one more independent variable. What would you suggest we add? (One answer is given at the end of the chapter)

Q: **Why is it that "statistics" is taught as a part of psychology (15)?**

A: Good question. It may seem strange that math should be part of a course dealing with the mind and behavior. In fact, many psychology departments require at least one course in statistics in order to graduate (my own department requires one course in statistics, one course in general research design, two courses in specialized areas of research design, and a first year math course in order to graduate with a 4-year degree in psychology).

The reason is that psychology is an empirical science. We are interested in studying the causes of behavior and the only way we can determine the causal factors is by conducting experiments. To do this, you need to know something about research design and something about how to interpret the results of studies.

This is where statistics comes in. One reason we need statistics is that people behave in a less predictable fashion than rocks (for example) and we need to increase the precision of our data in order to avoid making an error. We are always looking to see if our results could have occurred by chance. If so, our predictions are not supported and we must revise our thinking. But if the statistics indicate that it is unlikely that chance was a factor, we may be on to something.

Q: **What's the difference between the variance and the standard deviation (16)?**

A: The simple answer is "not that much". The standard deviation is simply the square root of the variance. Both provide an index of the variability in a distribution. In particular, we are looking at the degree of spread of the scores around the mean. In some distributions the various scores will differ quite a lot from the mean value, but in others the scores will be very similar. Consider distribution the following distributions:

A: 3,4,5,6,7 & B: 1,1,1,5,17

In each case, the mean of the distribution is 5.0, but the scores are a lot closer to the mean in distribution A as compared to distribution B. The variance is higher in A than in B. So why do we have two measures of variability? When you calculate the variance you end up with squared units values, not the original units. To fix this problem we take the square root and call it the standard deviation.

Q: **What does p <.05 mean? Please help (17)!**

A: In psychology, the outcome of an experiment (if favorable) does not "prove" a theory--the outcome supports the theory. This is partly because the scientific method recognizes the fact that nothing is certain--there is always an element of chance possible. The results might appear to support your theory by chance alone and we could end up making a mistake about the success of a treatment or the effectiveness of a drug.

The term, p <.05 , is a statistic indicating that the results of your study are estimated to be due to chance only five times in one hundred. Stated another way, the probability (p) that the results are due to chance is 5% (.05). Thus, we are 95% sure that the effect we are looking at is a real effect due to our experimental treatment. This is a standard cutoff level in psychological research. As scientists, we are willing to accept a 5% error rate in our studies. Note: you may see other error rates in a study, e.g., p <.01 would indicate a 1% probability that the results were do to chance factors.

Q: **Is it true that the person who "invented" the lobotomy was killed by one of his patients (18)?**

A: The idea of performing a lobotomy to calm violent behavior is attributed to a man named Egas Moniz. In 1935, he reported that a radical prefrontal lobotomy (i.e., removal of the prefrontal lobes) reduced violent behavior in chimps. This procedure seemed likely to be effective in controlling behavior problems in mental institutions, and over the next few years, Moniz performed several hundred lobotomies. They did seem to have a calming effect on some patients, but there were numerous side-effects such as a blunting of all emotion, intellectual impairment, and the possibility of death (about 4% of the patients died). Nonetheless, the procedure caught on rapidly and over the next few decades, in excess of 40,000 people were lobotomized. Part of the attraction of the procedure was its simplicity (it could be performed on an outpatient basis). There were also no effective drug treatments available for mental disorders until 1952. Moniz received the Nobel prize for Medicine in 1949.

Moniz was attacked and shot by a patient, but the

patient was not lobotomized, and Moniz was not killed in the attack (he was paralyzed).

Q: **Who was Stanley Milgram (19)?**

A: Stanley Milgram will be remembered as one of the great figures in the field of social psychology. He was born in New York in 1933. He graduated from Queens College in 1954 and worked with both Solomon Asch and Gordon Allport as a graduate student. Following graduate school, he was appointed to Yale. His work with Asch was on conformity to majority group pressure and this area intrigued him. At Yale, he turned his attention from the judgment of line lengths (the procedure used by Asch) to something a little more powerful— obedience to authority. He knew that people would conform when group pressure was directed toward opinions or visual discriminations, but would people really follow the group when someone's safety was at stake? Milgram's classic studies indicated that they indeed would. Sixty-five percent of the participants in Milgram's experiments obeyed the authority figure (the experimenter) and delivered (or so they thought) a 450-volt shock to an older man in the next room.

Milgram was very much interested in how "real people" reacted in "real" situations. He pursued applied topics and work in the field, looking at everything from our reaction to "familiar acquaintances" (people we recognize, but don't really know), to our experience of living in the city, to helping behavior. Stanley Milgram died in 1984. For a nice collection of his works, see The Individual in a Social World (1977), published by Addison-Wesley.

Q: **I was reading about the Milgram experiment the other day and wondered why the participants did not just leave. Isn't it the case that anyone is free to leave a study at any time (20)?**

A: You are absolutely correct. According to the ethics guidelines of the American Psychological Association (APA), any participant in a research study is free to leave at any time during the experiment for any reason at all. Terminating the study is not to result in any penalty for the participant, and the individual should be awarded any credit that would have been given for a completed experiment. However, these guidelines were not in place at the time that Milgram conducted his famous experiments on obedience. In fact, it is partly because of the reaction to the Milgram experiments that APA moved toward the creation of ethical guidelines, complete with the establishment review boards at the various institutions. It is quite unlikely that an experiment like Milgram's would be approved by an ethics board today.

Q: **When writing in APA style, is it O.K. to put the running head in question form (21)?**

A: Absolutely. Here's what the APA style manual says about running heads:

"The running head is an abbreviated title that is printed at the top of the pages of a published article to identify the article for readers. The head should be a maximum of 50 characters, counting letters, punctuation, and spaces between words. Type the running head flush left at the top of the title page in all uppercase letters." (APA Manual of Style, Fourth Edition, 1994)

It is quite O.K. to ask a question. For example the running head for this particular question might be:

CAN THE RUNNING HEAD BE A QUESTION?

Whenever you have a concern about writing style, always refer to the APA style manual. A copy should be available in your local library. To access some frequently asked questions about writing research papers see www.apa.org/journals/faq.html

Q: **I've heard people use the term "et al." after someone's name when they're talking about research. What does this mean (22)?**

A: The term et al. is from the Latin et alii, meaning "and others". Whenever there are multiple authors on a research paper, e.g., Smith, Jones, Nelson, & File (1999), we often refer to the paper as having been written by Smith et al. (1999) for convenience. Note that this convention applies to papers written by more than two authors: We would **not** refer to a paper by Smith and Jones (1999) as Smith et al. (1999).

Q: **What would you add to the study on caffeine and learning (23)?**

A: There are a number of possible second independent variables to add to the study (yes, you can have more than one independent or dependent variable). A good choice in this situation would be to look at the possible effects of drinking coffee per se on learning. The original study is set up to examine the effects of caffeine on learning. However, the way we administer the caffeine is by having people drink coffee. Might there be some effect of just drinking coffee (with or without the caffeine) on learning? To examine this, we could have two other groups drink decaffeinated coffee (either five cups or two cups) while reading. If it is the caffeine by itself that affects learning, then only the first set of subjects will show the predicted results.

Biopsychology: Foundations of Behavior

Why bother with all this "biology stuff" in a course on Psychology? Why should it matter that you know how a neuron works? Good questions. Sometimes it seems like the first few chapters in a psychology text are foreign and you might begin to wonder if you bought the right book. But we need to understand how the nervous system works in order to fully comprehend how our thoughts and feelings are shaped by the world around us. Depression is as much a biochemical event as it is a negative explanatory style -- both factors make us feel "depressed". In addition, many of the interesting things we want to know about will require some biological knowledge. For a full appreciation of psychology, we need to understand behavior at all levels.

Q: **What does all of this physiological stuff have to do with psychology (1)?**

A: Many students wonder why they should learn about neurons or the parts of the eye in a course dealing with human behavior. First of all, remember that psychology is often defined as the science of the mind and behavior. Psychologists are interested in scientific explanations of how the mind works and functions and how behavior is acquired and maintained.

Given this broad interest, psychologists will look for information in a variety of species (not just humans) and at a variety of levels. This brings me to the second point. In order to understand behavior you must examine it from a number of standpoints. Let's look at an example. What causes aggression? Perhaps you might answer "anger" or "frustration." Well it is the case that angry or frustrated people are more likely to be aggressive. But this answer is only part of the explanation. At any given moment, it may be that external circumstances can trigger an aggressive response. However, some cultures allow for the display of aggression more than others. So we need to consider the broad cultural context in which the frustration occurs. Also, some people handle frustration better than others. Do they have more will power? Perhaps... but they may also have a different baseline level of arousal and are not as easily ticked off. We should keep in mind that damage to certain brain areas may result in heightened aggression, as will an imbalance in body chemistry. The question "what causes aggression" can be answered on a number of levels, and to really understand what causes aggression, we should be familiar with all the answers.

Q: **What is a seizure and how can it treated (2)?**

A: A seizure refers to a period of sudden over-activity of the neurons in the cortex. If the cells in the motor cortex are activated, a convulsion (extreme, uncontrollable muscle activity) will likely follow. Individuals who have grand mal seizures resulting from epilepsy will also experience a convulsion. The cause of seizure disorder is likely to be brain damage resulting from an injury or stroke, but viral infections and various drugs may bring on a seizure as well. Treatment of seizure disorders typically involves anticonvulsant drugs such as Dilantin. These drugs work by blocking excitatory post-synaptic potentials, and may increase the effectiveness of inhibitory connections. Most disorders respond fairly well to medication and no further treatment is necessary. However, in extreme cases, surgery is necessary to remove the damaged brain tissue. In even more extreme cases, the corpus callosum may be severed to prevent the seizure activity from spreading from one hemisphere to the other-resulting in the "split-brain" situation.

Q: **What does the spleen do (3)?**

A: The spleen is a fist shaped organ located on the left side of the body just under the diaphragm. You might think that the spleen, like the appendix, was relatively useless since we tend to remove it whenever it is ruptured.

While it is true that an individual can live quite well without a spleen, they tend to be much more susceptible to blood infections. It would appear that the spleen is a filtering site for bacteria and other invading cells. There is a high concentration of both T-cells and B-lymphocytes in the spleen that detect any non-resident cells, match them against known invaders, and produce antibodies if appropriate. The spleen also will remove dead cells and other debris from the blood.

If the spleen has been removed, the individual is up to 50 times more susceptible to infection, particularly diseases such as pneumonia and malaria. The risk is greatest for children and falls to about eight times higher for adults.

Q: **What if a neuron doesn't have enough "firing power" (4)?**

A: Neurons produce an action potential (they "fire") in an all-or-none fashion. The situation is analogous to pulling the trigger on a gun. If sufficient pressure is applied to the trigger, the firing pin is released and the gun fires. In a neuron, the "pressure" on the trigger is actually a change in internal electrical charge (the neuron depolarizes). With sufficient depolarization, the threshold level is reached (the "trigger"), ion channels in the cell membrane open, and positively charged sodium ions rush into the neuron. The result is a rapid change in electrical potential from negative to positive: the neuron has "fired." So, it's not the case that a neuron would not have enough firing power, but it may be the case that the threshold has not been reached. Perhaps stimulus intensity was too weak, or perhaps the neuron has a very high threshold. Note that several sub-threshold stimuli can add together and the combined depolarization may be sufficient to "fire" the neuron.

Q: **What's the difference between an action potential and a graded potential (5)?**

A: This question illustrates a point that many students find confusing. Communication in the nervous system reflects a combination of electrical and chemical activity. The neuron basically is a tiny chemical battery with a semipermeable membrane. Inside the membrane are a number of electrically charged particles called ions (in particular, sodium, chlorine, potassium, and an organic anion). There are ions outside of the membrane as well (sodium, chlorine, and potassium).

The membrane is semipermeable--it has holes in it that allow some of the ions to move freely from the inside to the outside and back again. Because some of the ions are too big to pass through the holes and the concentrations of the various ions are different on the inside versus the outside, the neuron ends up with an electrical charge or resting potential of about -70 millivolts (a millivolt is 1/1000 of a volt).

When the neuron is stimulated, an interesting process begins. The neuron starts to **depolarize**--it becomes less negative. One of the results of this depolarization is that sodium channels open in the cell membrane and sodium ions (which are positively charged) begin to enter the cell. The neuron is becoming more positive. At a certain level (around -50 millivolts), the firing threshold is reached and the sodium channels open wide. Potassium rushes into the cell as well. Very quickly, the neuron acquires a positive charge (about +40 millivolts).

Over the next few milliseconds, the positive ions leave the inside of the cell either by diffusion or they are "pumped" out. The electrical charge once again, becomes negative. As the neuron "recycles", it actually overshoots the resting potential by about 20 millivolts, and then returns to -70 millivolts. This entire process (going from -70 millivolts to +40 millivolts and back again) is the action potential. Note: Neurons either "fire" (change from negative to positive) or they do not. The generation of an action potential is an all-or-none phenomenon.

Not so with a graded potential. A graded potential is the change in electrical activity in the dendrite of a post-synaptic neuron. When one neuron communicates with another, it does so by a chemical messenger called a neurotransmitter.

These chemicals attach to the dendrites of the receiving neuron at specific sites. The effect is to change the electrical activity in the dendrite. If the dendrite becomes more positive, we refer to it as depolarization (actually, we call it an excitatory post synaptic potential or EPSP). If the dendrite becomes more negative, it reflects hyperpolarization--the result of an inhibitory post synaptic potential or IPSP. EPSPs and IPSPs are graded. You can have a little bit or a lot. They add together as well so that an EPSP and IPSP of equal strength will effectively cancel the signal. The graded potential gradually spreads to the cell body and if the EPSP is of sufficient strength, an action potential will be generated at the axon.

Q: **What is serotonin (6)?**

A: Serotonin (or more technically, 5-hydroxytryptamine or 5-HT) is a neurotransmitter found in the human nervous system. Chemically, it is similar to both norepinephrine and dopamine and has been implicated in learning, memory, thermoregulation, sleep, and hunger. In fact, serotonin is one of the most diverse neurotransmitters around.

Researchers have discovered at least four different types (with several subtypes) of serotonin receptors on the post-synaptic membrane, each producing a different behavioral outcome. Serotonin also seems to be involved in a variety of psychological disorders including anxiety, obsessive-compulsive disorder, schizophrenia and depression.

Antidepressants such as Prozac, Paxil, or Zoloft act to selectively inhibit the reuptake of serotonin following synaptic transmission. The result is that more of this neurotransmitter remains in the synapse, acting on the receptor sites.

Q: **What is a migraine headache (7)?**

A: There are many different types of headaches. Tension or muscle headaches are experienced as a dull band of pain on both sides of the head. They may be caused by poor posture, eyestrain, or emotional conflicts such as grief or depression. Tension headache is the most common type of headache and is typically treated with over-the-counter medications.

A migraine headache tends to produce a throbbing pain, often quite severe, and is generally localized on one side of the head. Often accompanied by nausea, vomiting, and dizziness, migraines affect more than 23 million people in North America. Women are three times more likely than men to have an attack.

Migraines are associated with increased blood flow in the arteries and veins surrounding the brain as well as with changes in the level of serotonin. About one-third of migraine suffers will report the presence of an "aura" between 5 and 30 minutes before the migraine begins. This aura may involve visual experiences such as wavy lines or flashing lights or visual or auditory hallucinations. The presence of an aura may indicate neurological problems and you should seek medical attention.

Stress, fatigue, or too much caffeine or alcohol may cause a migraine. Food additives such as nitrates, or specific foods containing tyramine (such as red wine, aged cheese, pickled foods, or peas) may also contribute to migraines. The drug, propranolol, (a beta-blocker) is sometimes prescribed to relieve migraines. You should always check with your family doctor if you experience recurring headaches of any kind.

Q: **What is a brain tumor? What are some of the side effects? And if you have surgery, what are the chances of not having anything wrong with that person (8)?**

A: This is a difficult question to answer because it depends on the kind of tumor and where it is located. A tumor is a mass of cells growing at an uncontrolled rate and serving no useful purpose. The tumor may be relatively harmless (benign) or it may be cancerous (malignant). Even a benign tumor can be problematic if it exerts undue pressure on the brain. Tissue can become compressed and, consequently, cells will die or fluid flow may be interfered with. Thus, a complete neurological assessment is necessary to determine the location, rate of growth, and the predicted problems it will cause. With this information, a decision can be made about an operation.

Will surgery "fix" everything? Again, this is hard to tell with complete confidence. If the tumor is benign, removing it will reduce the pressure on the brain, but it is difficult to assess what damage has been done. A malignant tumor not only exerts pressure, but may metasize—spread to other areas of the brain or body, so there may be complications. As with any medical decision, it is important that you seek advice from a qualified professional (e.g., a neurosurgeon). Your family doctor can help to interpret the information and refer you to the appropriate people.

33 Ask Dr. Mike

Q: **We saw a tape in class about removing half of the brain. Is that half left empty or is something placed in the skull to balance the brain (9)?**

A: Some type of filler may be used if a large enough portion of brain tissue is removed. A small lesion would not require any external filler- glial cells would "fill in" the space. However, if a larger portion were removed, you would have to repack the gap. There is a product available for this, a kind of spray foam that expands to fill the cavity.

Q: **I read a story the other day about the "motor map" of the brain shown in most textbooks being wrong. What's the story (10)?**

A: Most introductory psychology texts and many upper level medical/neurobiology books have a diagram of the motor cortex based on the work of Penfield in the 1940s. The diagram shows the topographic organization of the motor area-a literal mapping of various body parts onto the surface of the primary motor cortex. This "motor homunculus" shows an orderly progression from the toes upwards through the body to the head and face.

However, this diagram, used for more than 50 years, does appear to be wrong! The original diagram was constructed by applying a mild electrical charge to the surface of the brain during surgery for epilepsy. Dr. Philip Servos stimulated areas of the face and measured the response using functional Magnetic Resonance Imaging. He found that the plotting of the face in Penfield's map was upside down. It is not the forehead that is close to the hand area, but rather the chin. Servo suggested that the original measuring instruments were not really precise, and that the artist who drew the original diagram may have exercised some "artistic license".

Q: **What is the cause of ambidexterity (11)?**

A: Handedness (the preference to use one hand over the other) is species-specific. In humans, about 90% prefer to use their right hand. What does this mean? Recall that the human brain is divided into a right and a left hemisphere. Typically, the left hemisphere in humans is dominant. We're not really sure why the left rather than the right (or both) becomes dominant, but probably it reflects the early fetal environment, particularly hormonal factors.

Since the left hemisphere controls the right side of the body, people with left hemisphere dominance will be right-handed. For left-handers and for those who are ambidextrous (can use both hands with the same level of skill), the right hemisphere tends to be dominant.

Interestingly, language, which typically is the province of the dominant hemisphere, is equally likely to reside in either the left or right hemisphere for non-right-handed people. Those who are left-handed or ambidextrous also tend to have a thicker corpus callosum (the bundle of fibers joining the two hemispheres).

Q: I was just reading that "...in right-handed people the major functions of language are carried out in the left hemisphere." I've never seen the reference to "right-handed" before so, does anyone know if left-handed people have major language functions carried out in the right hemisphere (12)?

A: One of the distinguishing features of cortical processing is the lateralization of the function you mention. It turns out that the left hemisphere "controls" the right side of the body, while the right "controls" the left side of the body. (In vision, this contralateral control is reflected in the right and left visual fields, not the right and left eyeball). Furthermore, each of the hemispheres seems to handle specific tasks, e.g., the left hemisphere is specialized for language while right tends to dominate in the processing of nonverbal information.

This lateralization is true for most of us, and an easy index is handedness-people who are right-handed (about 90% of the population) will have language localized in the left hemisphere. But what about the other 10% of the population who are either left-handed (or ambidextrous)? There is no clear-cut pattern. Some show language abilities in the right hemisphere, some in the left, and some in both.

Q: What is a "split-brain" procedure (13)?

A: In a case of severe epilepsy, it may be necessary to cut the corpus callosum in an effort to prevent the spread of the disorder. In the 1960s, two neurosurgeons, Philip Vogel and Joseph Bogen, discovered that cutting the corpus callosum reduced seizures in epileptics that had been deemed untreatable. Epilepsy will typically involve a focal site located on one hemisphere only. Thus, by severing the major communication link between the hemispheres, there is no route by which the disease can move to the second hemisphere. Since the major line of communication is cut, the procedure is often referred to as a "split-brain" procedure-the two hemispheres are functionally disconnected.

This sounds like a pretty radical thing to do. The corpus callosum contains approximately 200 million axons--cutting it should result in a profound effect on the individual but it does not. You would have a difficult time identifying a split-brain patient except under very particular circumstances. For example, if you restrict visual information to one hemisphere only, the individual may not be able to identify the information.

Have a look at the diagram. An individual is looking straight ahead at a fixation point (in the middle) on a screen. A word is flashed on the screen very quickly. In this case, the word is "treetop". The visual pathways are organized such that everything to the right of the fixation point will go to the left cerebral hemisphere and everything to the left of the fixation point will travel to the right cerebral hemisphere. If you ask the person what word they saw, an individual with an intact corpus callosum will say "treetop". The corpus callosum allows for communication between the hemispheres. The two pieces of information ("tree" and "top") are integrated and the left cerebral hemisphere--where language functions are localized--can give the correct answer. However, a split-brain patient has a severed corpus callosum. The information cannot be shared by the two hemispheres. If you ask a split-brain patient what they saw they will answer "top". This is the only piece of information available to the left, verbal hemisphere. So when asked for a verbal response, the left hemisphere has to answer using the only information it has available.

If you were to ask for a nonverbal response, the right hemisphere may be able to answer. For example, if the patient was shown a number of objects and asked to point to the object flashed on the screen using his left hand, he would point to a tree. The left hand is controlled by the right cerebral hemisphere and when asked to respond in this fashion, the right hemisphere uses the information available to it--the word "tree". Curiously, the patient would appear somewhat confused after pointing to the tree. The left hemisphere would become aware of the choice, and "realize" that the object being pointed at was not the one it remembered!

TREE·TOP

Q: Does the research on "split-brain" patients suggest a basis for the unconscious? Is the left hemisphere conscious, while the right is unconscious (14)?

A: Interesting question. Is it the case that consciousness resides only in one hemisphere? It is interesting to note that the fibers of the corpus callosum do not fully mature until about one year of age, so perhaps the hemispheres are operating somewhat independently at first. However, most authors would suggest that consciousness is an integrated phenomenon, incorporating the operation of both hemispheres, and our ability to reflect on those processes.

But what about the split-brain patients? Recall that these patients have had their corpus callosum severed in an effort to prevent the spread of epilepsy. Do they have two brains or two identities? No. A split-brain patient is almost impossible to detect without very sophisticated lab equipment. They function exactly as the rest of us, unless you can isolate information to one or the other hemisphere. It is only then that you can observe the split-brain effect (e.g., being unable to report verbally on information presented only to the right hemisphere). For more information on consciousness, see the article by Crick and Koch in the September, 1992 issues of Scientific American, or the article by Chalmers in the December, 1995 issue.

Q: What would happen if someone with Parkinson's disease took cocaine (15)?

A: Parkinson's disease is a movement disorder marked by involuntary shaking, weakness, and difficulty in initiating movement. The cause is a depletion of the neurotransmitter, dopamine (DA), particularly in a region of the brain called the substantia nigra . Patients with Parkinson's are often treated with L-DOPA, the precursor for DA, and this does result in an improvement of the symptoms.

Cocaine is a stimulant that blocks the re-uptake of DA. Recall that synaptic transmission involves the release of a neurotransmitter into the gap between an axon and a dendrite. After the neurotransmitter has diffused across the gap and locked into the receptor sites, remaining molecules are reabsorbed back into the axon terminal to be used again. Cocaine blocks this re-uptake process in systems where the neurotransmitter is DA (norepinephrine as well). In essence, the released molecules of DA remain in the gap and continue to stimulate the post-synaptic receptor sites. The psychological experience is a "high."

So will this help a person with Parkinson's disease? Probably not. Cocaine merely prevents re-uptake of DA - it does not create additional molecules. The Parkinson's patient has very little DA to begin with, and preventing re-uptake will have little if any effect.

Q: Does marijuana act as an antagonist or agonist? My friend said that it is an antagonist because it acts as a neurotransmitter and binds to a receptor. She also said that because the THC in marijuana acts as an antagonist, it can make your brain function slower which lowers your IQ. But my boyfriend says that marijuana makes you smarter because the THC "coats" your neurons, which causes you to think harder about things. Who is correct (16)?

A: Let's start by defining some terms. Almost all drugs work at the level of the synapse by altering the action of specific neurotransmitters (or by mimicking their action). Drugs that facilitate the action of a particular neurotransmitter are referred to as agonists, while those that inhibit action in some way are called antagonists. Note that we are classifying the drugs on the basis of their effects--a drug can be an agonist for one neurotransmitter and an antagonist for another. In fact, a drug could have different action for the same neurotransmitter at a different synaptic location.

So is THC (tetrahydrocannibinal) an antagonist or an agonist? In order to answer the question, we must consider what THC does at the synaptic level, and what the normal neurotransmitter would be.

THC is in the class of drugs known as hallucinogens. Many hallucinogens (e.g., LSD) act as serotonin antagonists, releasing the inhibition on neurons that control REM sleep and dreaming. But THC is not a serotonin antagonist. Rather, THC binds to specific THC receptor sites in the brain. So, your friend is correct in saying that THC binds to receptors, but it is not an antagonist.

Incidentally, the effect of THC is to produce mild sedation, make you feel hungry, reduce blood pressure in the eyes (which is why it is often used to treat glaucoma), alter perception, and interfere with concentration. It does not "coat" your neurons and you will perform more poorly on cognitive tasks while under the influence of THC.

Q: **I am reading this book about a famous psychiatrist who sexually abused his patient under the influence of amytal. Have you ever heard of this case? What is amytal and what is it used for? What are the effects of long term use (17)?**

A: Amytal is a barbiturate. The full name of the drug is sodium amytal or amobarbital. Typically, it is given to reduce anxiety (a tranquilizer), but may be prescribed for sleeplessness, tension, and other anxiety-related disorders. Barbiturates are depressants and as such, slow brain activity. In fact, amytal may be used to control convulsions and if injected directly into the carotid artery, it will shut down hemispheric activity. Long term use can lead to dependency and high doses can be lethal. I believe that the case you mention involves one Dr. Masserman--a very well known psychologist who treated patients with amytal and sexually abused them while they were sedated. The amytal would also help to block any memory of the incident.

Q: **What is an antihistamine and how does it work (18)?**

A: Histamine is a neurotransmitter released following tissue damage or when foreign particles such as pollen enter the body. The effect is to constrict the large blood vessels and dilate the smaller ones. One immediate result is a blockage of air passages, headache, and lowered blood pressure.

An antihistamine is a chemical compound from the class of drugs called depressants (this category includes drugs such as alcohol, codeine, and morphine). Antihistamines prevent histamines from functioning properly. Most work by blocking histamine receptor sites at various tissues and organs. Thus, symptoms of histamine functioning, such as a stuffy nose are reduced.

Q: **What can you tell me about the drug, "ecstasy" (19)?**

A: Ecstasy is a designer drug, i.e., it is created by changing the molecular structure of an existing substance. Technically, its chemical name is methylenedioxymethamphetamine (MDMA). Methamphetamine is more commonly known as "speed". Ecstasy is both a stimulant and an hallucinogen. Thus, it will have some of the same effects as cocaine (a stimulant) and consciousness-altering drugs such as LSD. Effects include euphoria, alertness, a disruption of hunger, sexual behavior, changes in sensory perceptions, etc.

Ecstasy is common in the rave scene where people may want to stay alert and euphoric for hours. The effects are generated by increasing the release of serotonin and dopamine, and by also blocking the re-uptake of these neurotransmitters. Combined with hours of non-stop dancing, there is a risk of exhaustion and dehydration when taking this drug. Designer drugs in particular can be very dangerous. Since they are synthetic, one must place a lot of trust in the "designer".

Q: **What are the effects of PCP on the brain (20)?**

A: PCP is the drug phencyclidine, or more commonly, angel dust. It was developed as an anesthetic about 50 years ago, but quickly taken off the market due to the side effects. It is classified as an hallucinogen like LSD, but unlike LSD does not produce its effects by interfering with the action of serotonin. PCP binds to glutamate receptors (glutamate is the most abundant excitatory neurotransmitter found in the brain), effectively blocking them. The result is symptoms similar to schizophrenia: hallucinations, rigid stare, emotional withdrawal, and even catatonia.

You may have heard of glutamate before as the compound, MSG (monosodium glutamate). MSG is a flavor enhancer added to many prepared foods. While approved for use, it has become somewhat controversial. Certain individuals may experience an adverse reaction, ranging from increased asthmatic symptoms to dizziness and numbness.

Q: **What is Luvox (21)?**

A: Luvox is one of the trade names for the drug, Fluvoxamine Maleate. It is typically prescribed for the treatment of obsessive-compulsive disorder (OCD). OCD is an anxiety disorder where an individual has an unwanted, recurring thought (the obsession) and feels that they must engage in some type of repetitive behavior (the compulsion) in order to ward off or rid themselves of the thought. Luvox also may be prescribed for other types of anxiety disorders (e.g., panic attacks) or for the treatment of depression.

Luvox is a selective serotonin re-uptake inhibitor or SSRI. Other SSRI's include Prozac and Zoloft. Following the release of neurotransmitters into the synaptic cleft, the axon of the pre-synaptic membrane will "reabsorb" some of the chemicals in a process called re-uptake. Luvox inhibits this process, effectively leaving more serotonin in the synapse. This will result in increased communication between the two cells and relief from the symptoms of OCD or depression.

Q: **What is Ginkgo? Does it improve memory (22)?**

A: Ginkgo Biloba is a tree native to central China. The leaves are harvested and dried and used as an herbal preparation. The primary use is to improve circulation and it seems to have some success in the elderly population. However, it does not seem to affect a normal, healthy individual. Ginkgo also seems to affect the utilization of glucose within the brain, with the effect of increasing alertness. This property in particular suggested that Ginkgo may be useful in the treatment of Alzheimer's Disease. Indeed, clinical trials indicate that Ginkgo (in large doses) is effective in slowing the progression of Alzheimer's.   But once again, any effects on a normal healthy, individual are questionable. For more information on Alzheimer's Disease and its treatment, check out the Alzheimer's Society online at www.alzheimers.org.uk

Q: **Is there a chemical in turkey that makes you sleepy (23)?**

A: Many people notice that they become sleepy following a Thanksgiving feast. Is turkey the culprit? Turkey does contain the amino acid tryptophan that converts to the neurotransmitter serotonin in the body. Serotonin has been implicated in mechanisms of sleep. However, the amount of tryptophan in a slice or two of turkey is not enough to produce sleepiness. The need for a nap is more likely related to the large meal (rich in carbohydrates) you consumed along with the turkey.

Sensation & Perception

The second set of biologically oriented chapters in most texts involves the sensory systems. Although students find the material on perception quite interesting, the physiological details of the visual system seem foreign. A common question in the sensation chapter is "How much of this do you expect us to know?" It is difficult to provide an answer that will be general enough for all courses, but I think that a focus on function is good advice. In addition, most texts devote more space to the visual system than to the other sensory systems—chances are that the visual system will receive more attention at exam time. There are many interesting demonstrations that can be done in class for perception, and many questions reflect student interest in these processes. There are also numerous questions that people have wondered about for a long time, and they will arise in this chapter. Was mom right--do carrots really improve your eyesight?

Q: **What do glasses do (1)?**

A: In order for us to see clearly, a visual image must be precisely focused in the retina. Recall that the retina contains the light-sensitive detectors called rods and cones. The accurate focusing is accomplished by accessory structures in the eye, notably the cornea and the lens. If there are problems with either of these structures, the image will not fall on the retina, and our vision is blurred. An image focused in front of the retina results in the condition known as nearsightedness or myopia. If the image is focused behind the retina, the condition is called farsightedness or hyperopia. Glasses can correct the problem by refocusing the image so that it once again falls exactly on the retina. As we age, the muscles controlling the lens (the cillary muscles) weaken, and we are more likely to require glasses to correct the problem.

Q: **Are carrots good for your eyesight (2)?**

A: Actually, they are. Most plants contain beta-carotene, a chemical that plays a role in photosynthesis. Beta-carotene is an important component of Vitamin A, and Vitamin A is responsible, in part, for the production of rhodopsin. Recall that rhodopsin is the visual pigment found in rods and it breaks down in the presence of light. People with a Vitamin A deficiency do not produce enough rhodopsin and, consequently, have poor rod vision (a syndrome often referred to as night blindness). Increasing Vitamin A intake—perhaps by eating carrots—will help the situation.

Q: **What happens when your eye becomes "blood-shot" (3)?**

A: The redness observed when you eye is blood-shot is due to tiny blood vessels in the outer covering layer of the eyeball. Sometimes, these blood vessels become infected or irritated due to lack of moisture, or they may swell due to an allergic reaction. The symptoms typically can be relieved by taking an antihistamine, which reduces the swelling.

Q: **When older people begin to have problems with their vision, does this have anything to do with damage to the visual cortex (4)?**

A: Typically not. It is always possible that some kind of damage to the primary visual cortex may have occurred, but this is not the usual reason that our sight becomes worse as we grow older. The most common reason reflects an inability to focus a clear image on the retina. One problem is a weakening of the ciliary muscles-the muscles that control the shape of the lens. Under normal conditions, the lens is adjusted in order to focus the image as sharply as possible on the retina (a process known as accommodation). As we age, the focusing is incomplete, and we may need glasses to help with the process. Other common problems include a loss of shape in the cornea or the eyeball itself, and cataracts-a condition in which the lens becomes cloudy or milky and light will not pass through.

Q: **What's the difference between additive and subtractive color mixing (5)?**

A: Look at the wall in front of you. What color is it? Whatever your answer, the wall appears to be a particular color because of the light waves that are reflected from the wall back into your eye. The paint (pigment) on the wall absorbs some of the wavelengths—the pigment subtracts these wavelengths from the full compliment available in white light leaving you with an impression of color. If you mix another paint color with the one already on the wall, you will subtract out another set of wavelengths to achieve the resulting color. On the other hand, an additive color mixture is achieved when you mix colored lights rather than paint pigments. If you shine two colored lights on a screen, they will mix together (add) as they are reflected back to your eye. With an additive mixture, it is possible to match any color using just three wavelengths—one from the short end of the spectrum (violet), one from the long end (red), and one from the middle (green).

Q: **When light enters the eye and hits the retina, does it strike the receptors right away (6)?**

A: Strangely enough, no. The retina consists of several layers of cells. When light reaches the retina, it first encounters the ganglion cell layer, then the bipolar cell layer, and finally, the receptor layer (there are few other cell types, e.g., horizontal cells running between the layers). So the image must "pass through" all those outer layers of cells before it even reaches the light-sensitive receptors. As you can imagine, the image is pretty fuzzy at this point and needs to be sharpened and enhanced for further processing.

Q: **What actually happens during laser eye surgery (7)?**

A: Two of the most common visual problems are nearsightedness (myopia) and farsightedness (hyperopia). In both cases, the image is not focused precisely on the retina. With myopia, the eyeball itself is typically too long and nearby objects are seen more clearly than those in the distance. The opposite is true for hyperopia—the eye is too short and objects in the distance are seen more clearly. Glasses or contacts correct the problem by increasing or decreasing the focal length, bringing the image into sharp focus on the retina.

Focusing in the eye is accomplished by the cornea (the transparent covering) and the lens. While the lens "fine-tunes" the focus, the bulk of the job is handled by the cornea. This is where laser surgery come in. The idea is to adjust the focus by reshaping the cornea. The first step would involve a detailed mapping of the eye to get a precise idea of how much adjustment was necessary. During the surgery (LASIK or **La**ser-In-Situ **K**eratomileusis), a flap is shaved off of the cornea (about 25% of the cornea's thickness). This flap is bent back and a very precise laser is used to reshape the corneal tissue to the desired curvature. The flap is then replaced and the patient is given eye drops to lubricate the eye and to prevent infection. The entire procedure takes about five minutes per eye.

Laser surgery has become very popular and while safe, it is not without risk (which is the case for any type of surgery). For the LASIK procedure the risks vary from minor pain following the procedure (about 1 in 50 cases) to a more serious infection of the corneal flap (about 1 in 5000 cases). In addition, the procedure may result in an undercorrection or an overcorrection with the result that the patient must still wear glasses or contacts. For more information see the report in the July-August 1998 issue of *FDA Consumer Magazine*. The article is available on-line at www.fda.gov/fdac/features/1998/498_eye.html

Q: **Why can you sometimes still see flashing lights or "spots" after you shut your eyes (8)?**

A: While light is the primary stimulus for vision, it is not the only way to stimulate the visual receptor cells. The rods and cones in your eyes can be stimulated mechanically. Recall that the eyeball itself is filled with a viscous fluid called the vitreous humor. Pressure on the front of the eyeball is transferred to the back of the eye where we find the retina. This pressure causes the visual receptors to fire. If you close your eyes and press gently, you will begin to see random flashes of light that result from this mechanical stimulation. So, when you close your eyes tightly, the pressure results in a visual experience. Remember that the eyelid is somewhat translucent and a certain amount of light will also pass through and fire the receptors.

Q: **Why do your ears get "blocked" and "pop" when landing in an airplane (9)?**

A: This is basically the result of unequal air pressure on the two sides of your eardrum. The middle ear contains the eardrum, the ossicles (three small bones), and air pockets behind the eardrum. Under normal circumstances, the air in the pockets is being constantly replenished through the Eustachian tube (a small passage connected to the nose). This keeps the air pressure more or less equal on both sides of the eardrum.

If the Eustachian tube is blocked for some reason (e.g., when you have a cold), the pressure drops because air in the pockets is absorbed by the lining of the middle ear. Since the pressure is lower behind the eardrum, it will be pushed inward. This results in abnormal vibration of the drum and sounds will be masked or muffled. The pressure will also feel uncomfortable.

A similar problem results when landing in a plane. Even though the cabin is pressurized, the rapid change from an area of low pressure to high pressure near the ground causes unequal pressure on the two sides of the eardrum. You simply do not have enough time to move the air through the Eustachian tube and "re-pressurize" the middle ear. This sensation can be quite unpleasant.

Is there anything you can do about it? The

American Academy of Otolaryngology recommends that you increase your swallowing (chewing gum helps here), yawn, or if your ears remain blocked, pinch your nose, take a mouthful of air and, using only your cheeks and mouth, blow through your nose. The "pop" you hear will indicate that you have been successful in re-balancing the middle ear pressure. It is critical that you do not use excessive pressure (e.g., do not use your lungs—if you do, you can damage your eardrum.

Q: **Does time really go faster as you get older (10)?**

A: It sure does seem that way sometimes! Time as a physical entity is more or less fixed—it doesn't really speed up as we age. However, our psychological perception of time may change. According to one theory of time perception, we gage time on the basis of the number of anchors or events between any two points. As the number of events increase, so does our perception of time. For example, what did you do last Friday morning between 9:00 a.m. and 12:00 noon?

Let's say that you went to school (event 1) had a class from 10:00 to 11:00 (event 2), then met some friends for lunch at 12:00 (event 3). I got into the office at 9:00 (event 1), had an appointment at 9:15 (event 2), a committee meeting at 10:00 (event 3), another appointment at 11:00 (event 4), met with my teaching assistants at 11:30 (event 5), then met a friend for lunch at 12:00 (event 6). As we reflect on our mornings, it seems to me that time blew by—I accomplished six things that morning. Perhaps, you feel like you had a pretty leisurely morning. For me, time moved fast, while for you time moved more slowly. As we grow older, it is more likely that we will have more events to fit in a given time interval, thus, we feel that time moves faster.

Q: **Why do you sometimes feel that the eyes of a person in a painting are "following" you (11)?**

A: The eyes don't really follow you, but it seems that way. An artist who wants to convey this illusion will take advantage of the fact that we tend to look at the eyes of another person when we speak to them. In fact, two people will look directly into each other's eyes about 30% of the time during a casual conversation. Eye movement recordings indicate that we seek out and attend to features of the face such as the eyes and mouth when we first glance at another person (live or in a photograph). So, in effect, we create the illusion that the eyes of the person in a painting are following us because we tend to make eye contact with the painting whenever we look at it. Artistic techniques can enhance the pupils so that it appears the person in the painting is looking back.

Q: **Do cartoons appear to move through the autokinetic effect (12)?**

A: Not through the autokinetic effect, but you're close. The autokinetic effect generates apparent motion. If you look at a stationary light source in a dark room, it will appear to move. The amount of perceived movement varies from person to person, but typically, the estimates from participants are in the range of 1 to 5 inches. This effect is due in part to the involuntary eye movements (saccades) and lack of a frame of reference in the darkened room. If your eye is moving, but there is no background to compensate for that movement, the result is the apparent movement of the light source.

Cartoons capitalize on a different apparent motion effect -- the Phi phenomenon. Imagine that you are looking at two light bulbs. Bulb A flashes, then a few moments later, bulb B flashes. If the time interval between the flashes is within a very narrow window (20 - 200 milliseconds), the perception is that the light "moved" from A to B. A shorter interval (under 20 msec.) results in the perception of simultaneous lighting of the bulbs, while a longer interval (over 200 msec.) gives the real picture--we see bulb A flash, go out, then bulb B flashes. The Phi effect is responsible for the apparent motion of lights around a theater marquee, and it can explain cartoons. If we move from one frame to another fast enough, we perceive continuous motion. In fact, this effect is behind any continuous video you see on your computer screen. It is being flashed at approximately 15 frames per second (a new flash every 75 msec.)

Q: **How do you explain those "magic eye" 3-D pictures (13)?**

A: The "magic eye" pictures actually work on the same principle as a stereogram. You've probably seen a stereogram before either when viewing the dessert menu at certain restaurants, or when watching scenes of a favorite cartoon character. You insert a disc containing small slide images into a viewing device resembling a pair of binoculars. The 3-D effect is quite startling.

But how does it work? Both stereograms and the magic eye pictures capitalize on a binocular depth cue called retinal or binocular disparity. Normally when we view a scene, objects at various distances project a slightly different image in the left and right eye. Hold your thumb about one inch away from your nose. Close one eye, and then the other. You will note that the view of your thumb changes depending on which eye you look at it with. The brain uses this disparate information to locate objects in depth. A stereogram "fools" the brain by presenting a slightly different view of a scene to each eye. The brain reconstructs the views, and objects appear at various distances.

The magic eye pictures do the same thing except each view is a very high contrast dot diagram of the scene. (You can view some images at www.magiceye.com.) Note that two images are actually presented. As you focus on the flat images, they appear to be just a swirl of dots – we are not getting any depth information. However, when you allow your eyes to un-focus, each panel presents a slightly different dot pattern to each eye. The disparity is integrated, and presto – an image appears.

Q: **Is pain a heightened touch reaction (14)?**

A: While this might seem reasonable, remember that there are many types of pain (e.g., a tooth ache) other than pain induced through touch (e.g., hitting someone). More importantly, the sensory receptors for touch are different from those for pain. A touch sensation involves several types of receptors, notably an onion-like receptor sensitive to changes in pressure called a Pacinian corpuscle. Pain does not seem to involve these receptors, but instead is detected by two types of fibers. A-delta fibers tend to have thick, myelinated axons and produce the fast, sharp experience pain. C-fibers are thin and unmyelinated and result in a slower dull pain. There are most likely other pain receptors, but these are the common receptors in the skin.

Q: **How does acupuncture work (15)?**

A: Acupuncture is a form of alternative medical practice and involves the stimulation of various points in the body (typically accomplished by inserting needles into these points). The ancient Chinese believed that the body is maintained by a vital energy source called the "Qi" (pronounced "chee"). This force flows freely in the body along certain pathways or meridians to the 12 major organs (loosely related to the organs we call the kidney, heart, etc.) If the Qi flows freely and in the correct strength, then the individual is healthy. However, when the meridians are blocked, we have an imbalance that results in illness. Acupuncture restores the balance by opening or closing the meridians as appropriate. This is accomplished by stimulating the pressure points, which may be far removed from the source of pain or discomfort.

Is there any evidence to support the effectiveness of acupuncture? Actually, there is. Various studies have demonstrated that acupuncture is more effective than either a placebo treatment or a "sham" treatment where needles are inserted at the incorrect points (see Vickers, 1996; and Johaansson et al., 1993). These studies suggest that acupuncture can be effective in the treatment of chronic pain and for the treatment of substance abuse. It is probably not beneficial in other situations, e.g., to help an individual stop smoking. How does it work? We're not entirely sure, but two factors are likely. First, the acupuncture pressure points are located such that stimulation of the points will excite A-Delta fibres. These particular nerve pathways are involved in pain perception and actively inhibit pain signals in the slower C-fibres. Second, it appears that stimulation of the pressure points results in the release of both endogenous opiates (endorphins) and the neurotransmittter serotonin. The result would be a suppression of pain.

Vickers (1996). *J. R. Soc. Med.*, *89*, 303 – 311.
Johansson et al. (1993*). Neurology*, *43*, 2189-219

Q: **We have been talking a lot in class about ESP. What is your opinion on this subject (16)?**

A: The notion of Extra Sensory Perception is intriguing. We all have an intuitive feeling that there must be something to this since we know people who are very good at predicting when events will happen or they seem to know exactly what we are thinking. The real question with ESP is how do we evaluate the claims made about it. If we want to consider ESP as a scientific issue, then we must subject it to scientific procedures. That is, we must conduct properly controlled experiments where the variables of interest are not confounded and there is no potential bias. Claims of ESP fail this test. Thus, from a scientific viewpoint, I have to reject the possibility of ESP.

Does this mean that ESP does not exist? No. It means that I cannot find scientific proof for its existence. Perhaps we have not done the proper experiment yet, or perhaps we simply do not yet have the technology or methods to properly assess ESP.

Q: **Why do we see "impossible" images (17)?**

A: Look at the fork-like image. What do you see? Are you sure that it's some object with 3 prongs? Look closely at the prong in the middle. Does it really exist?

This is an impossible figure. At first glance, the

drawing appears to be a three-dimensional object with three prongs to the right. But a closer inspection reveals that the middle prong is not really there. As you scan from left to right the prong seems to jump into visual awareness. And it can be very frustrating trying to ignore the illusion— it will not go away.

The figure is created by joining the wrong lines on the right hand side of the image. For example, the top prong should be rectangular and consists of the first three lines at the top. In the diagram, I've joined the first two lines only and used a circle rather than a rectangle. As we scan the image, we fail to take in all of the information at once.

Scanning the image makes "sense" to our visual system regardless of whether we scan from left to right or right to left. Consequently, we "create" the impossible figure by allowing the information from both sides of the image to be used. The result is an image that can not exist.

Note: you can help your visual system resolve the image by covering up either the right side or the left side of the figure.

Q: **What is backward masking (18)?**

A: Backward masking is an experimental technique in which a noise source or "mask" is delivered to a subject at some time after the original signal source was presented. For example, I might want to determine your ability to detect a tone (signal source) when noise is present (the mask). I would play tone and then follow it with a mask (e.g., a plane taking off). I could vary the intensity of the mask, the intensity of the tone, how long after the tone I present the mask, and so on.

The term has also been used to refer to messages recorded "backwards" in various popular songs. Some have claimed that rock groups used these back-encoded messages to promote drug use and their own particular political or moral agenda. While it is the case that tracks have been back-encoded, the data indicate that we simply do not perceive the "message" being presented. We may be aware that there is a back-encoded track, but we cannot report what, if anything, is being said. There is also no evidence that such messages are perceived "subconsciously" and influence our behavior.

Q: **I know that the moon can't really be bigger when it's just rising, but it looks that way. Why (19)?**

A: The "moon illusion" has been noted by many observers over the years and while they all agree that the horizon moon looks larger, there has been considerable debate over the exact cause of this effect. Early theories held that the effect was physical--the result of some kind of magnification of light rays at the horizon. More recent theories focus on a psychological interpretation. When we observe the moon at the horizon, there are a number of depth cues (such as linear perspective) provided by the earth's surface. These cues are not available when the moon is high in the sky. The depth cues on the horizon generate the illusion that the moon is further away than it actually is. At this point, our perceptual system "calculates" the apparent size of the moon. The perceived size depends on the perceived distance. The further away an object appears, the "larger" it seems to be. Thus, we re-scale the size of the horizon moon and perceive it to be larger than it really is.

Under normal circumstances, this principle makes a good deal of sense. Take a quarter and hold it about six inches in front of you. Now move it out to arm's length. Even though the actual size of the image on the retina is smaller at arm's length, we still perceive the quarter to be the same size—an effect known as size constancy. Here the retinal image is smaller at arm's length and we use the distance cues to re-scale the perceived size of the object. But in the case of the horizon moon, the retinal image is not smaller. Nonetheless, we use the distance cues, re-scale the size of the moon and generate the illusion.

Q: **When you're watching an old Western movie, why do the wheels on the wagons seem to be spinning backwards (20)?**

A: This is a motion after effect that works through a mechanism similar to that responsible for color after images and contrast effects. If you look at a spiral spinning in a clockwise direction for about 30 seconds and then shift your attention to a stationary target, the still image will appear to move in the counterclockwise direction! How can I explain this?

As you adapt to the moving image, you stimulate detectors for motion in the clockwise direction. At the same time, you actively suppress or inhibit neurons that would detect movement in the opposite direction. Once you stop the stimulation, it appears that there is more activity in the counterclockwise neurons than in the clockwise detectors. Thus, we perceive motion in the opposite direction. As you watch the wagons, you stimulate motion in one direction. But as you adapt, the image blurs and "becomes" stationary. At this point, we perceive motion in the opposite direction.

Consciousness & Motivation

This chapter addresses the issue of what makes us do what we do. Moreover, are we aware of the forces that drive us or is most of human behavior the product of some unconscious motivation? There are a number of very interesting issues that arise during a discussion of consciousness and motivation, but the one that generates the most questions is the topic of sleep and dreaming. By the time we reach the age of 72, we will have spent 24 years sleeping and 5 years of this time will be in the dream state of REM. What's going on here? Why do we sleep? What is the meaning of dreams (if any)? Can you control your dreams? I will try to answer some of these questions below. Note: You will find more questions and answers on dreams in Chapter 9 on Personality. There we will examine the perspective posed by Sigmund Freud.

Q: In what stage of sleep are people most receptive to suggestions and memorization? In other words, if one listens to something during sleep, in which stages will they be able to comprehend or remember it (1)?

A: An individual may be responsive to external stimulation during REM and possibly when talking in their sleep (a non-REM event).During REM, brain waves are very similar to the relaxed, awake pattern and the sleeper is likely to be dreaming.

External events (such as noises or water on one's face) may be incorporated into the dream. Note that the sleeper may take an external event and weave it into their dream-it is not the case that the sleeper is "suggestible" and that one can implant ideas about what to do when the sleeper awakes. In addition, the sleeper is not likely to "learn" while asleep. So the idea of memorizing material or learning a new language while asleep does not work.

Will the sleeper remember anything about the external event when they awake? Perhaps. Dreams are very fleeting experiences and we do not always remember them. However, if we do incorporate an external event into the dream, it may become more vivid or "real" to us, making it more likely that we will recall the dream when we wake up.

Q: **What are sleeping pills and how do they work (2)?**

A: Sleeping pills fit in the category of drugs called depressants. They reduce arousal levels and result in sedation or even a loss of consciousness. Most common prescriptions contain either barbituates or benzodiazepines (one of the most heavily prescribed drugs is called Diazepam-Trade name: Valium). Both types of drugs seem to work through GABA receptor sites. The action is a bit complicated, but when Valium is present, for example, the effects of the neurotransmitter GABA are heightened. The result is an increase in the level of inhibition. The effects can be increased dramatically if an individual on Valium consumes alcohol-this combination can be lethal.

65 Ask Dr. Mike

Q: **Can dreams predict the future? How do you explain the fact that sometimes you dream about something and then it happens (3)?**

A: The belief that dreams are predictive of future events has been with us since the dawn of time. Some cultures revere dreams and the ancient Egyptians used them to guide government decisions. Are they predictive of the future? No. There is no evidence to indicate that dreams give us a window on the future. So why does this myth persist? Perhaps it is the mystical quality of a dream, or perhaps it is simply the fact that we seem to dream about real life events that makes them appear meaningful. Or perhaps we fool ourselves.

Consider the following scenario. You are dreaming that an old friend really needs to speak to you and keeps phoning. You do not pick up the phone and some very important message is never transmitted. As you wake up, you realize that the phone is ringing and, to your surprise, it is the old friend in your dream! How can I explain that?

There are two points for you to keep in mind. First, remember that we tend to incorporate external events into our dreams, particular in the last REM period. So, if the phone is ringing, you may very well "add" it to your dream before you wake up. Second, we have a strong bias towards remembering events that confirm our beliefs. The fact that it was your friend is remembered and the dream appears predictive. However, you have conveniently forgotten all of those occasions when the phone was ringing and it was not the person in your dream at all.

Q: **Is it common to know that you are dreaming while you are in a dream (4)?**

A: It is not all that common to realize that you are dreaming and in a dream, although most people report that this has happened to them at some time. This situation is referred to as "lucid dreaming". During a lucid dream, the sleeper often reports that they felt as if they were watching themselves dream... sort of inside and outside at the same time. Steven Laberge at Stanford University has suggested that about 1% of the population are capable of lucid dreaming on a regular basis and that the onset can be aided by external stimulation (such as flashing lights to the eyes).

Q: **I've been told that if you fall from a high building in your dream and you don't wake up in time, you could actually die. Is this true (5)?**

A: Many people believe that if you fall in a dream and do not wake up in time that you will actually die. There is no evidence to support this, or any claim regarding people who dream that they "die". My guess is that this sort of dream generates a lot of arousal and we often will wake before "hitting" the ground. Because we wake up in an almost panic state, we assume that somehow our mind has protected us by waking us up before hitting.

Q: **Can you practice to have a lucid dream? How (6)?**

A: Lucid dreaming is a state in which the dreamer is consciously aware that he or she is actually having a dream. During a lucid dream, the dreamer may see himself or herself and try to exert some control over the content. Steven LaBerge (1985) claims that sleepers can, in fact, learn to control their dreams and have a more active say in what goes on. The key is to learn to recognize that you are dreaming. Most of the time, we are not aware that a dream is taking place. But if we know that we have entered this state, then we have a better chance of lucid dreaming.

LaBerge helps sleepers by giving them a signal during REM. Typically, the sleeper wears goggles that flash after a few minutes in REM. During REM, we are sensitive to external cues, and with practice, we can use this cue to trigger awareness. Note that this type of practice requires a sleep lab. It is difficult to signal REM in any other way, but some researchers suggest that if you go over what you want to dream about before going to sleep, you can help control the direction of a dream. The more practiced the script, the more likely it is that your dream will unfold in this manner.

Q: **Is it possible to walk or act out behavior while dreaming (7)?**

A: Actually, it is, but it is not very likely. Remember that dreams usually occur during REM sleep (Rapid Eye Movement). Normally, motor movement is suppressed during REM--the body is essentially "paralyzed". This is a good thing, because we are prevented from acting out the behaviors that occur in our dreams. But the inhibition may not be maintained indefinitely and movements can "escape" -- people may twitch or roll over when dreaming. Large-scale muscle movements (like walking), however, are not likely to occur. An individual who sleep walks does so in very deep stage of sleep (Stage 3 or 4), not during REM. Thus, it would be very unlikely to sleep walk while dreaming.

Nonetheless, there are reports of people who have done just that. In such cases, the dreamer was either not in REM at the time (while the vast majority of dreams occur during REM about 10% occur in other stages), or possible, had a sleep disorder. In males over 50 years of age, a REM-related movement problem can develop. The cortex fails to inhibit movement during REM and the dreamer actually does act out his dreams. This, of course, can be very problematic if the dream involves vigorous activity such as playing football.

Q: **Why can't you remember your dreams when you wake (8)?**

A: Why do we have such difficulty recalling dreams? First of all, let's remember that everyone dreams, every night, on several occasions. So it's not the case that some of us dream and others do not...we all dream. Dreams typically occur during REM sleep, and each of us will have 4 or 5 REM cycles per night. Periods of REM get progressively longer as the night goes on. The longest REM period occurs just before we wake up and can last almost an hour.

Dreams are fleeting images. According to the activation-synthesis theory, a dream is merely what happens when the cortex tries to interpret various electrical signals generated in the area of the Pons. We are not conscious while dreaming, but we are trying to make sense out of the neural activity.

O.K., so why can't we remember these dreams? Memory is enhanced by activities such as conscious attention, rehearsal, and actively integrating new information with old. We do very little of this while dreaming, thus, it is not really surprising that our memories for dreams are so poor. We will tend to remember very vivid dreams, and those that occur during the last REM period. Try keeping a dream journal. Write down everything you can remember about your dreams immediately when you wake up. I believe that you will find that you can write something almost every day, but will forget it before you finish your breakfast!

Q: **Do people in comas dream (9)?**

A: This is a tough question to answer because the standard method we use to determine when people are dreaming-waking them up and asking what was going on-is not available to us. However, we can look at the EEG recordings of people in comas and see if they resemble those of people who are asleep. A recent study published by Parsons and Crosby in Sleep Medicine Alert suggests that there are some components of sleep visible in the brain waves of comatose patients. People in a deep coma showed EEG patterns consistent with delta and theta waves-similar to periods of deep sleep. As the patients regained consciousness, the EEG patterns began to look more and more like standard sleep stages (although components were often missing). The last stage to return was REM sleep. So it would appear that people in comas show some brain wave patterns that resemble normal sleep. However, REM-like patterns were not seen when the patient was in a deep coma. Thus, it is unlikely that the patients were dreaming during this time.

Q: **Do dogs dream (10)?**

A: The answer is: I can't tell you for sure, but I'm willing to bet they do. Many, if not most, mammals experience periods of REM during sleep. We know from research with humans that REM sleep is associated with dreaming-eighty to ninety percent of all dreams occur during the various REM cycles. We find this out, of course, by attaching electrodes to people in a sleep lab, and waking them up at various sleep stages. If the individual was in REM, they are likely to report a dream. Animals are capable of remembering things, so it seems quite reasonable that when Rover is dreaming (probably about chasing a cat) when his eyes dart back and forth under the lids.

Q: **My eight-year old son is frequently waking up in a sort of "altered state". He is usually frightened as if from a "bad" dream. He tries to talk but his words are mostly incoherent. He'll talk using fragments of words, walk around his room and sometimes cry for about five or ten minutes. Then he'll suddenly yawn, lie down and go back to sleep. In the morning he remembers nothing of the episode. What's going on (11)?**

A: It sounds like your son may be experiencing "night terrors". This sleep disorder is characterized by a sudden awakening during sleep accompanied by screaming. The child will appear disordered and confused. The child will not report a dream or nightmare--this disorder is not related to REM sleep, but rather occurs during Stage 4 sleep (the deepest stage). Typically, the child will fall back to sleep a few minutes later and remember nothing in the morning.

The likely cause of night terrors is an abnormal timing cycle for sleep. Typically, we cycle through the various stages several times during the night and then wake up after a final pass through REM. With night terrors, the child suddenly wakes from stage 4 sleep. This can be very frightening for the child.

Most sleep disorders will disappear as the child grows older. Nonetheless, you should consult your family doctor.

Q: **What is narcolepsy? And can narcolepsy affect your sex life (12)?**

A: Narcolepsy is a sleep disorder in which the individual suddenly falls asleep at "odd" times. For example, an individual may be talking to you or driving a car and then suddenly, for no apparent reason, falls asleep. The onset of narcolepsy is associated with muscle weakness, so the individual will typically fall down if standing (one of the major problems with this disorder is hurting oneself when falling). While it would appear that the person is in a very deep stage of sleep, a narcoleptic attack usually begins with REM, suggesting that the problem may be caused by an abnormal REM timing cycle. Curiously, the onset of an attack may be triggered by strong emotions, so the individual with narcolepsy may indeed fall asleep when sexually aroused.

Q: **Why do people yawn (13)?**

A: Most of the time, people yawn because they are sleepy! But this does not have to be the case— people will yawn when they are bored too. What causes a yawn? One theory holds that yawning is the reflexive result of too little oxygen at the brain stem. Engaging in a yawn seems to increase arousal levels, which should result in a greater flow of oxygen. However, others have argued that yawning is not influenced by increased oxygen flow, nor is there a lack of oxygen in the blood of people who engage in excessive yawning. There is also some debate about the type of neurotransmitter involved.

The bottom line is that we do not have a satisfactory explanation at this time. Nonetheless, yawning seems to be a behavior that we frequently engage in. Yawning is not limited to humans, but seems universal throughout the animal kingdom (yes, your cat actually does yawn). And perhaps most interestingly, yawning seems to be contagious. Seeing someone yawn will almost assuredly generate a yawn in the observer. In fact, just talking about yawning can stimulate a response—just like the one you're having right now.

Q: **Dr. Mike, I've been having horrible nightmares for about a month. They started during the summer, so I don't see how they could be stress related. It's not one re-occurring nightmare; a lot of them are spin-offs from another one. Topics range from murder, shootings, kidnappings, snakes, clowns killing people, and other similar things. Most end with someone dying. Can you shed any light on this (14)?**

A: It is difficult to pin down why someone has any particular type of dream ...nightmare or otherwise. Remember that dreams are the result of our cortex interpreting neural signals from lower brain areas and this interpretation may reflect events during the day, things that are of concern to us, or nothing at all. Let me assure you that nothing unusual is happening -- the dreams are not premonitions of future events nor are they the result of someone trying to contact you. My guess is that for some reason you started dreaming about these events and they disturb you; so much so that you continue to think about them during the day and consequently, the same type of dream reoccurs that night. As with most dreams, you are merely incorporating your daily thoughts into your nighttime activity.

Can I offer any advice? You might try to alter the outcome of these dreams by "rehearsing" how they should unfold during the day. Imagine a different, more positive outcome and go over this scenario in your mind. In this way, you are likely to use this new interpretation when the dream begins again. If you are still concerned about the dreams, consult your family doctor or a local psychologist. They can offer more advice on the issue.

Q: **What can you tell me about Rohypnol (15)?**

A: Rohypnol (also known as "roofies," "rouche," "R-2," or "rope") is the common name for the drug Flunitrazepam. It is a very powerful antianxiety drug in the same family as Valium (a benzodiazepine), but it is about ten times stronger than Valium. This drug is illegal in both the United States and Canada, but is often manufactured and prescribed in Europe and Mexico. Apart from the fact that it can be addictive, Rohypnol can cause dizziness, blackouts, and memory loss. Recently, Rohypnol has been involved in a number of date rape cases. The drug, when added to a victim's drink, is virtually undetectable since it has no odor, color, or taste. The result is a very fast "high," followed by the symptoms of intoxication, and, finally, passing out. Rohypnol is a dangerous drug. When mixed with alcohol, it can result in breathing problems and death.

Q: **What is THC and how does it work (16)?**

A: THC is the abbreviation for delta-9-tetrahydrocannabinol – the active ingredient in marijuana. Marijuana is classified as a hallucinogen. Low doses can produce perceptual distortions, while high doses can result in hallucinations, delusions, a loss of touch with reality, and a high level of sympathetic nervous system activity. THC binds to specific receptor sites in the basal ganglia, hippocampus, cerebellum, and cortex.

THC (along with other cannabinoids in marijuana) is psychoactive (i.e., produces an effect that alters perception) but it is not a narcotic (such as heroin). Physiological effects include increased heart rate, dilation of the blood vessels in the eye (this reduces pressure in the eye and is the reason marijuana may be prescribed to relieve systems of glaucoma), sedation, and a stimulation of appetite.

Q: **Does alcohol really kill brain cells (17)?**

A: In a sense this is correct. The active ingredient in alcoholic beverages (ethyl alcohol) is classified as a depressant and has a number of effects on the body. At low doses, the result is sedation, motor impairment, and disinhibition. At higher does, alcohol can decrease the activity of neurons, which may result in coma and death.

Alcohol binds with GABA receptors, increasing the activity of this inhibitory neurotransmitter. In addition, it can both increase and decrease the effect of glutamate, and reduces the flow of calcium across the neural membrane. Alcohol effectively destabilizes the cell membrane and interferes with cellular processes. The result can be a non-functioning cell. Long-term usage of alcohol can produce severe brain damage and condition known as Korsakoff's syndrome.

Q: **What is a "lie detector" (18)?**

A: A lie detector is a physiological recording device called a polygraph. Typical measures of arousal taken would include heart rate, breathing rate, skin temperature, and galvanic skin response (the skin's ability to conduct an electrical current). The lie detector does not detect lies at all, but rather records physiological changes in response to questions asked by the examiner. The theory is that someone who is guilty will show a greater physiological response when asked critical questions about a crime, compared to control questions. Those who are innocent should show much less arousal to critical crime-related questions. In fact, we might expect an innocent person to show more arousal to the control questions, since they typically involve questions about activities where we expect mild transgressions (e.g., "up to the age of 18, did you ever deceive anyone?").

Is this an accurate way to detect deception? Surprisingly, the polygraph is not as accurate as you might expect. Many studies indicate that the overall accuracy rate is about 70%. But this does not tell the whole story. In one study, expert judges reviewed the polygraph records from 50 real cases where the suspect was innocent (another person confessed later) and 50 cases where the suspects later confessed that they did commit the crime. Results indicated that 75% of the guilty suspects where caught by the polygraph experts, but 39% of the innocent suspects were also tagged as guilty. To put this in perspective, imagine that 1% of the students in my introductory psychology class cheat on the next exam. There are 1200 students in the class, so that means if 12 actually cheated, the lie detector would catch 9 of them and suggest that 463 others are in trouble too!

Q: When I get angry, why does my chest start to hurt (19)?

A: Most likely, you are experiencing the effects of heightened arousal. When you experience anger, there is an associated increase in arousal... heart rate goes up (more than any emotion except fear), and skin temperature increases more than any other emotion. You probably start to breath faster as well. In your case, you are probably sensitive to changes in arousal level, and consequently, you note that your chest "hurts". In actuality, you are breathing faster and your heart rate is up.

Q: I am unclear on the specifics of an anxiety attack/disorder. I find myself sweating (palms, armpits, and feet) quite a bit. Not only when I'm in public, but sometimes when I'm completely alone. I somehow get a little nervous around people, but I don't feel it all the time. Would you say this is related to anxiety (20)?

A: Everyone experiences anxiety and arousal from time to time. Symptoms such as increased sweating, increased heart rate, etc. would be typical. The thing that sets these normal reactions apart from a diagnosed clinical problem is the severity of the reaction, the length of time it is experienced, and the irrationality of the stimulus situation promoting the attack. Consider a Panic disorder. Individuals who suffer from Panic Disorder will experience sudden, intense feelings of fear that can last for hours. The fear is not brought about by frightening stimulus... it just happens. They may feel sick to their stomach, dizzy, experience chest pains, choking sensations, etc. In general, they are terrified and feel as if they will die. In extreme cases, the individual may develop agoraphobia- they avoid going outside of their house so that they do not have to worry about having an attack in public. If the persistent sweating you report continues or becomes more frequent for no obvious reason, consult your family doctor.

Q: **What is actually measured when someone measures your "arousal level" (21)?**

A: When someone talks about your arousal level they are referring to the level of activity in your autonomic nervous system (ANS). The ANS is composed of two branches, the sympathetic nervous system and the parasympathetic nervous system. In general, the sympathetic system is involved in gearing the body up for action, while the parasympathetic system does the opposite—it quiets the body and conserves energy. When the sympathetic system is activated, the result is increased heart rate, increased breathing rate, and dilated pupils. Parasympathetic activation results in decreased heart and breathing rate, constricted pupils—the opposite of whatever the sympathetic system does. Typically, arousal level will be measured on a recording device called a polygraph. Standard measures include heart rate, breathing rate, and galvanic skin response (the electrical resistance of the skin).

Q: **Can a polygraph really determine whether or not you're lying and how could I do a demonstration on lying in the classroom (22)?**

A: As mentioned earlier, a polygraph measures changes in physiological activity such as heart rate, skin temperature, galvanic skin response (GSR), etc. They are very good at detecting changes in autonomic nervous system arousal, but not "lies". This is why lie detector tests, while used in many investigations, are not permitted in the courtroom—

you can not 100% determine that the arousal changes are due to lying.

What kind of demonstration can you do? A good one is to see if people are able to detect deception in others. Most people believe that they are quite good at detecting lying, but the data indicate otherwise. Overall, the accuracy rate for detecting truth or deception is only about 55%. When we look at other people we think we know what the cues to lying are, but like the polygraph, those cues may be associated with something else.

You might bring two people to the front of the room and ask them some questions (where were they born; what did they do last Saturday night, etc.). Each person will get a different question (2 each). The questions are on a piece of paper in an envelope and right under the question is an instruction to either tell the truth or to lie. They should read the question to the class, and then answer it (either truthfully or with a lie). Tell the class that their task is to determine who was lying and who was telling the truth for each question. After the demonstration, you can talk about the cues that people use to detect deception such as breaking eye contact, pausing or hesitating when answering, using a lot of "um's" in their speech.

Have fun!

Q: **My friend and I have a bet and hope you can settle it for us. Who is better at lying, men or women (23)?**

A: When it comes to nonverbal behavior and the ability to display (encode) or detect (decode), the data are fairly clear—women are "better" in most situations. Women are superior to men in the accuracy with which they display nonverbal signals of emotion and they decode emotional cues more accurately as well.

With respect to deception, women are better at nonverbal deceit, and they are more likely to be able to detect lying in others. Apparently, women pay more attention to subtle nonverbal cues. When you make the nonverbal display "leakier" by focusing attention on channels other than the face, the difference is minimal. It is most difficult to detect deception from the face because of our ability to control facial muscles very precisely. Other areas (such as the body) are more difficult to control and thus "leak" more nonverbal information.

Q: **Are facial expressions reflexive (24)?**

A: Many authors have suggested that facial expressions in humans have indeed evolved from basic reflexive actions. Consider the emotional display for "disgust." The characteristic facial cues for this emotion are a raised upper lip, tightened eyebrows, furled forehead, and flared nostrils. This display may have developed from the desire to block one's nose in the presence of a foul odor (pressing the upper lip in an upward direction will do this). Similarly, an anger display (open mouth, bared teeth, open nostrils, squinting around the eyes) could reflect the facial movements necessary to increase air flow and narrow the field of vision in an emergency situation.

This makes sense, but not all facial displays are reflexive in origin. Consider the smile. Sometimes smiling is linked to happiness (a reflexive action), but at other times we smile for social reasons (e.g., when meeting people on the street). Thus, we must consider the context when interpreting any nonverbal cue.

Q: **I've heard that there are only six emotions. Is this true (25)?**

A: Not really, but... We've all experienced the sending (encoding) and receiving (decoding) of emotional facial expressions. It seems that there are very specific cues related to a particular type of emotion. Paul Ekman (1971) set out to examine the types of facial expressions that were universally understood—those that would be easily decoded by people all over the world. He showed photos of North Americans displaying a variety of expressions and asked people from various cultures (including a tribe from New Zealand who had basically no contact with North Americans) to identify the expressions.

He found that there were six emotions that could be readily identified: happiness, fear, anger, sadness, surprise, and disgust. Ekman termed these the primary emotions. Are these the only emotions? Of course not. There are many others we might identify such as love and joy. Some are culturally specific and some may reflect a mixing or "blend" of two primary emotions. But the six primary emotions are the ones that are easily identified all over the world.

Q: **What is the significance of eye contact in human interaction (26)?**

A: In North American culture, we place a great deal of importance on the eyes in social interaction. We even have eye-related sayings in our language (e.g., "making eyes at" and "look me in the eye when you say that"). In a typical interaction between two acquaintances, each person will spend about 70% of the time gazing at the other person, and about 30% of the time engaging in mutual eye contact. The average length of an eye contact episode is about 2 seconds, and if it lasts longer than 7 seconds, we may find the interaction unpleasant. Such staring results in physiological arousal. What function does eye contact serve?

At a basic level, there is an information seeking function—this is a method by which we can gather visual data about someone else. In many animal species, prolonged eye contact is an aggressive signal, and we humans probably react in the same way. But in between aggression and information, eye contact is related to attraction. We will look longer at people (or objects) that we like. Close friends will engage in more eye contact than strangers will. In fact, we will tend to like those who look at us longer, as long as staring does not occur.

Q: **It seems to me that people spend a long time looking up at the floor indicators in an elevator. What's going on (27)?**

A: Good observation! It does seem that people spend a lot of time looking up at the floor indicator in an elevator. Are they really that concerned about missing their floor? Probably not. A more likely explanation involves the discomfort experienced by the close interaction distance in the elevator.

Most people in North America have a spatial preference of about two to four feet when interacting with a stranger. This is a comfortable space for us. Closer interaction distances result in increased arousal—we get uncomfortable when a stranger is standing only inches away. Argyle and Dean (1965) suggested that one way to deal with this arousal would be to compensate and reduce any arousal from other nonverbal channels. Eye contact represents an easy way for us to do this. Most people engage in eye contact when interacting, but not for very long. Prolonged gazes (e.g., over seven seconds) increase arousal and we will again feel uncomfortable.   So we can reduce our overall level of arousal in the elevator by looking away. The floor indicator provides a convenient target for our gaze. Note that we could compensate by moving away, but this is much more difficult in an elevator.

Q: **Can meditation heal ,e.g., diseases, depression, etc. (28)?**

A: The answer is "yes", meditation may in fact have an effect on various diseases. The real problem is determining how and why. One of the goals of meditation is to relax, to achieve alpha rhythm. There may be other aspects as well, e.g., improved physical health, better diet, spiritual connection, etc. All of these togetheʀ (or in isolation) may be able to "heal". We just can't say how it might work psychologically. Perhaps taking time to reflect on your problems will help you to overcome them. Perhaps your changed life style will improve your health. Or perhaps any improvement is do to effort justification. Cooper (1983) demonstrated that snake phobias could be helped by either a traditional treatment (implosion) or by riding an exercise bike--as long as the patient freely choose the treatment. If we believe that certain behaviors might be useful and we spend a lot of effort in doing those behaviors, we will justify our effort and come to believe in the success of the treatment. This belief may be all that's necessary for a cure.

Q: **What types of things can be "cured" with hypnosis (29)?**

A: Hypnosis is not so much a cure, but rather an aid to some other treatment used by a therapist. One way in which hypnosis may play a part is to help achieve relaxation during systematic or in vivo desensitization. Another use would be to help an individual "loosen" their repression of some memory they find too painful to bring into conscious awareness. Note: if you are interested in exploring the use of hypnosis for some clinical issue, contact your local clinical hypnosis society or the psychological association in your state or province. Do not look in the phone book under "hypnotists"!

Learning & Memory

The learning chapter turns out to be one of the more difficult ones in an introductory textbook. Perhaps it is because of the increased emphasis on theory. The previous chapters (usually biopsychology and sensation/perception) tend to be viewed as more "mechanical". One of the hardest concepts seems to be reinforcement. The distinction between positive and negative reinforcement is not as obvious to students as it is to instructors. Memory is closely related to learning. After all, to learn something suggests that we will be able to remember it. Learning and memory were often considered together back in the days when the dominant perspective in psychology was the behaviorist approach.

Q: **Why does a moth fly toward a light (1)?**

A: Some organisms have very basic motivational systems called taxes. A taxis is an orientation reflex that moves an organism toward (positive) or away from (negative) a particular stimulus. Such responses typically have survival value—organisms that display such behavior are likely to survive and reproduce. The moth has a positive phototaxis, and will fly toward a light source. Most of the time this works just fine, unless the light source is an open flame or one of those electronic bug killers. In contrast, the cockroach has a negative phototaxis. It will move away from any light source, which is why they scurry away if you turn on the lights at night!

Q: **Can learning occur "unconsciously" as suggested in "learn while you sleep" tapes (2)?**

A: Not really. For complex learning to take place (such as learning another language), you need to be consciously aware of the stimuli. However, this is not to say that no learning can take place without complete awareness. Marcel (1983) demonstrated that research participants showed a "semantic priming" effect even when priming words were presented too fast to register in consciousness. Others have demonstrated that we may prefer certain melodies that were presented frequently (also below threshold), even if we have no memory of ever hearing them. Thus, we do learn something without awareness, but it is highly unlikely that we could learn complex cognitive processes such as language or psychology in our sleep.

Q: **Can reinforcement be presented "subconsciously"? Can we learn without being aware (3)?**

A: Let me deal with the second question first. It is possible to learn without being consciously aware of the reinforcement in an operant procedure, or without being aware of the stimuli in a classical procedure. For example, let's say that we are talking and every time you say a plural noun, I reinforce that behavior by nodding my head and saying "good." Soon, you will be using many plurals in our conversation. Learning has occurred, but it is unlikely that you were aware of the reinforcement. But what if the reinforcement is presented subliminally to the unconscious mind? Will learning occur?

No, but you still might learn something about the reinforcer. Several experiments (e.g., Marcel, 1983) have shown that subliminal presentation of word cues does result in a particular effect called semantic priming. You will not remember the word, or even whether you'd seen it before the cue was presented below threshold. However, the time required for you to decide whether a follow-up string of letters is or is not a word is far shorter if the string has some semantic (meaning) relationship to the subthreshold cue. Clearly some material gets in even though we are not aware of it at all.

Q: **Do animals imitate? If so, what does this mean (4)?**

A: Yes, they do. Some animals, for example, chimpanzees, will imitate human behavior. If you stick out your tongue, they will too! A chimp will even respond to the "rouge test". This is a test designed to measure a child's sense of self-identity. Take a young baby (3 months old), put a dab of rouge on his or her forehead, and place the baby in front of a mirror. The baby will smile and laugh, but will not attempt to touch its forehead. The child is not aware that she is seeing self in the mirror. Older children (around 18 months) will touch their foreheads, indicating that they are aware that it is an image of self in the mirror. The fact that a chimp responds in much the same fashion suggests that chimps, like humans, have a sense of self.

Q: **How would a behaviorist explain the operation of an aphrodisiac (5)?**

A: You might assume that aphrodisiacs are completely unlearned and, therefore, not open to a behaviorist interpretation. First of all, we should note that a behaviorist does not necessarily have a problem with any behavior that may be "hard-wired." The fact that organisms eat when they are hungry and that this motivation is unlearned is not a problem for behaviorists. But behaviorists would want to consider what the organism eats and the circumstances that surround the feeding ritual - these can be (and probably are) learned. Let us assume for the moment that aphrodisiacs exist. Can we explain the attraction from a behaviorist perspective?

Sure. The aphrodisiac would probably be pheromone-based, so we could suggest that the smell is an unconditioned stimulus that produces a pleasant and arousing unconditioned response. The conditioned stimulus is the person wearing the aphrodisiac, and the conditioned response is a positive reaction toward that individual. Perfume manufacturers count on this conditioning to take place as often as possible. Are there such things as aphrodisiacs? Well, that's another question.

Q: **If you punish a response (e.g., bar-pressing), what happens when you no longer deliver the punishment (6)?**

A: First of all consider what happens when we deliver the punishment. Let's say that we have a rat in a Skinner box pressing the bar. We would like the rat to stop. So, whenever the rat presses the bar, we deliver an electric shock to the floor of the cage. Fairly soon, the rat will stop bar pressing. Thus, the result of delivering punishment is a decrease in the response strength of the behavior prior to the punisher. With a strong enough punisher, or after repeated trials, the behavior will cease. So, what happens when we stop delivering the punishment?

In general, we will get an extinction curve. The

behavior will cease for a while, and then may slowly return. Bar pressing is not normally an important behavior, so it may cease for quite some time. However, if the behavior is highly desired it could return quickly. For example, if the rat had to press the bar to get food, then bar pressing is likely to return when shock is discontinued. This partially explains why punishment in isolation is not a very good technique for behavior change. If someone is performing a desired behavior, they may stop as long as the punishment is in effect, but remove the punishment and the behavior quickly returns.

Q: **Do counterconditioning procedures ever backfire – with a transfer of fear to the positive stimulus (7)?**

A: Yes, it's possible. Counterconditioning is a behavioral therapy aimed at replacing an unwanted behavior with a more desirable or appropriate behavior. This type of treatment is often used when dealing with a phobia. Remember that a phobia is an acquired, irrational fear of an object. For example, perhaps you were once bitten by a dog and now you cannot be in the same room with any dog. Even the thought of a dog increases your arousal level. In classical conditioning terms, the general stimulus of a dog has become the conditioned stimulus for your conditioned response of fear.

To treat this phobia, we could try to replace your fear response with a more positive reaction. Let's say that you really like chocolate very much. So, I bring you into the treatment room and there is plenty of chocolate around as we start just talking about dogs. At the next session, I might show you a picture of a dog, but again there is lots of chocolate around. As the sessions progress, we eventually would bring a dog into the room as you relaxed with your favourite chocolate. In effect, I have paired the dog (CS) with the chocolate (UCS) and over time, the dog itself will elicit the same positive response as the chocolate (CR). Note that the procedure begins with a very weak version of the feared object and a strong version of the positive stimulus.

Across sessions, we gradually increase the strength of the feared object. This is essential in counterconditioning. If you were to start the first session with the real dog in the room, the fear would be so great that the chocolate would have no effect. In fact, the fear could transfer to the chocolate and you might end up hating both.

Q: **In Pavlov's studies, wouldn't he have trouble controlling the dogs as soon as they entered the experimental room? Wouldn't they learn to salivate at the sight and sound of the door (8)?**

A: Absolutely! The animals in Pavlov's studies not only learned to salivate at the sound of a bell or metronome, but did salivate upon entering the room. Over time, the door to the room (or the trainer himself) becomes a conditioned stimulus for food in the same way that the bell becomes a conditioned stimulus.

Those of you who have pets will know this effect very well -- your dog or cat will come to associate your behaviors with feeding. Even the sound of the can opener will generate a conditioned response.

Q: My dog has severe reactions to thunderstorms. He shakes, pants, and appears to be in a state of panic. Lately he reacts the same way to cars, trucks, and even rain on the roof. The vet prescribed an antianxiety medicine, but is there a nonmedical way to treat my dog (9)?

A: The first thing to consider is that your vet may have prescribed medication for a number of reasons, some not directly related to the "panic attacks." So, be sure to ask your vet why he prescribed the medication. Nonetheless, your dog's reactions are classic signs of phobia acquired through classical conditioning. Your pet acquired a conditioned emotional response to the sound of thunder, a response that has now generalized to other stimuli that are associated with, or sound like, thunder. Some form of behavior therapy might be a good alternative treatment for your pet.

Q: My students have a tough time in distinguishing between negative reinforcement and punishment. What are some good examples of each (10)?

A: I agree -- this is one of the difficult concepts for students when they hit the Learning chapter. First, let's remember the critical distinction between reinforcement and punishment: reinforcement will increase behavior strength and punishment will decrease behavior strength. Thus, anything that promotes the continuation and strengthening of behavior is a reinforcer, while something that results in a decrease in behavior is a punisher. In addition, a negative reinforcer involves the removal of something that the organism does not like, while punishment involves the delivery of a negative, disliked stimulus. Here are some examples:

A rat is given electric shock each time presses a bar. Soon bar pressing decreases. The shock is a punisher.

A rat in a Skinner box experiences foot shock (the floor is electrified every time a red light comes on). If the rat presses a bar, the foot shock will stop. Bar pressing increases and foot shock is a negative reinforcer for the bar press response.

A child is harshly scolded by his parents whenever he reaches under the kitchen sink to grab the cleaning solutions. Soon the child stops reaching under the sink. The scolding is a punisher for the reaching response.

A child fails to clean up her room and Mom and Dad take away her allowance. Soon the child learns to clean up her room. The removal of allowance is a punisher (something positive was removed).

John and Mary had a fight, and Mary refuses to speak to John until he says he is sorry. After a while, John can not stand the silence, and he apologizes. Mary's silence was a negative reinforcer for the apology.

Q: **What should you do if your dog runs away... punish him for running away or reward him for coming home (11)?**

A: Good question, and one that applies to more than our pets. Research has shown that reinforcement is most effective if it is delivered immediately. In shaping behavior, we want to strengthen the bond between a particular response and the consequences. Reinforcement can be delayed, but not for very long in most cases (e.g., no longer than 15 or 20 seconds following the behavior). If we wait too long the organism will have performed another behavior and we end up reinforcing something other than the one we want (this can explain superstitions by the way).

So punishment is not likely to be effective in this case—the behavior occurred too long ago. In fact, the punishment would be counterproductive in that you would be associating the return home with a negative experience. I would reward the dog for coming home.

Q: **What's the difference among desensitization, counterconditioning, and aversive conditioning (12)?**

A: These three approaches are all behavioral treatments based on principles of learning. Systematic desensitization is based on extinction. The idea is that we can expose an individual to a feared stimulus and with repeated exposure, that stimulus will cease to elicit the fear response. But to do this safely, we have the individual approach the situation slowly, first imagining what the feared stimulus looks like, then moving to thoughts of interacting with the feared stimulus and perhaps touching it, and so on. At each stage the individual is taught to relax and ease his fear. Eventually, the stimulus is no longer feared.

In aversion therapy, we want to reduce the performance of a behavior by providing a very negative consequence. For example, one treatment for alcoholism is to give the person a drug ("antibuse") that will make them quite sick if they consume alcohol. After a few exposures to such treatment, people want to avoid the illness, and consequently, they stop drinking. Note that this procedure depends on the individual taking the drug. Another way to avoid the illness is to stop taking antibuse—which explains much of the relapse in this type of treatment

In counterconditioning, we attempt to break conditioned stimulus-conditioned response bond by replacing it with a second more positive association. Let's say that you are afraid of books. To help you, I would start by identifying a very positive stimulus, for example, chocolate, if it is something that you really like. Next I'd ask you to think about a book and present you with a real piece of chocolate. It is important to present the feared stimulus at a relatively low level and the positive stimulus at a relatively high intensity. Over time, we will build up a positive association between "books" and "chocolate"—the books will no longer be feared.

Q: I've heard that the "box" theory of memory, with sensory, ST and LTM being clearly divisible in terms of duration, capacity, coding and forgetting mechanisms is no longer valid. Can you please tell me what has replaced this theory (13)?

A: "Box" theories of memory offer a useful analogy to the information processing system, but do not tell the whole story. A more recent view of memory is offered by the "levels of processing" hypothesis suggested by Craik and Lockhart (1972). The essential notion here is that material is more likely to be remembered if it is processed in depth rather than at a superficial level. A superficial level of processing (shallow processing) would look at surface characteristics of material (e.g., color, size, etc.). Deep processing involves a consideration of word meaning and semantic characteristics.

Note that this distinction is not incompatible with the box model. Short term memory "works" through the shallow processing mechanism of maintenance rehearsal (e.g., repeating the words to yourself). To get this into long term memory we need to perform elaborative processing (e.g., thinking about what the word means, how it fits into concepts you already know, etc.). Craik and Lockhart felt that attention was critical in their model--whatever you pay attention to will be remembered. So if I focus on surface characteristics, I will tend to remember these surface items, while deep processing generates a more elaborate memory.

Q: **Can the environmental context influence memory (14)?**

A: Memory is indeed context-dependent. Material learned in one context is best remembered in the same context. For example, Gordon Bower has demonstrated that material learned while subjects are happy is recalled better if subjects are happy during the recall phase. Similarly, material learned in one location will probably be recalled best if you are asked to remember it in the same location. For example, Godden and Baddeley (1975) had scuba divers learn lists of words either 10 feet underwater or on the beach. Next they were asked to recall the lists either underwater or on the beach. Thus, we have four groups: those who learned underwater and recalled underwater, those who learned on the beach and recalled on the beach, and two groups with a mixed learn/recall experience. The data indicated that recall for the word lists was greater if the context remained the same. Students often report that they feel more confident writing exams in the same room in which they heard the lectures. Indeed, exam scores are often higher when the same location is used.

Q: **What is synesthesia (15)?**

A: Synesthesia is a mixing of sensory modalities. Information presented to one sensory system (e.g., vision) gets coded in several senses. Individuals with synesthesia report that they "hear" colors or "taste" sounds in addition to the primary sensory experience. Individuals with synesthesia tend to have remarkable memory capabilities. Since the information was coded in a number of ways, retrieval is enhanced.

Perhaps the most famous case of synesthesia was reported by Luria in his 1968 book, The Mind of a Mnemonist. Luria describes the case of Shereshevski, a Russian reporter whose phenomenal memory skills were legendary. Shereshevski reported visual experiences upon hearing tones, and the intensity of the visual experience was related to the level and pitch of the tone. Often, a taste experience would accompany these visual experiences as well. Luria's account is fascinating and the book is well-worth reading (a 1987 updated version is available). The cause of synesthia is not exactly known, but the hippocampus is involved and there seems to be a genetic tag. It is more prominent in females and those who are not right-handed.

Q: **Could Beethoven's ability to write music after his deafness be attributed to the joining of senses, i.e., synesthesia (16) ?**

A: I have not heard that suggestion (although the composer Scriabin did make such a claim). In Beethoven's case, it is likely that his extreme familiarity with music allowed him to envision the process in his mind. He could continue to write music after his deafness because he could still compose even though he could no longer get external auditory feedback.

Q: **Does anxiety and/or stress affect recall on test performance (17)?**

A: There is not an easy answer to your question. Stress or anxiety can certainly interfere with performance on tasks. High levels of stress are distracting and will result in attention being taken away from the task at hand. Lower levels of stress may also interfere with performance, or in some cases, may actually improve performance. It depends on how complex the task is and how familiar you are with it. If the task is simple, or if you know it very well, then arousal can facilitate performance. But if the task is complex or it is new to you, arousal will inhibit your performance. Robert Zajonc describes this effect in his theory of Social Facilitation. You may also want to look at the Yerkes-Dodson Law. This law describes the relation between task difficulty, arousal, and performance. Basically, there seems to be an optimum level of arousal for peak performance on various tasks. For a very difficult task a moderate level of arousal is necessary for peak performance— easy tasks require a higher level of arousal.

Q: **Does dementia lead to Alzheimer's disease or is it a separate disorder (18)?**

A: As we grow older we face the possibility of senile dementia, literally an "undoing of the mind." Dementia is a natural result of the aging process. For example, we may become more forgetful or react more slowly to certain stimuli. Although, senile dementia shares many of the same symptoms of Alzheimer's disease, Alzheimer's is a very particular type of disorder.

Alzheimer's disease is a brain disease typified by progressive deterioration of thinking, language, memory, and eventually physical abilities. Alzheimer's affects about 5% of the population over 65 years of age and almost 30% of people in their mid-eighties. The first sign is a progressive memory loss. The individual may forget appointments and names. Recent events in the person's life start to fade next (what does this suggest about memory?), and ultimately, older, more established memories will fade. In the final stages, individuals may be bedridden and unable to help themselves. Alzheimer's is a terminal disease that can only be diagnosed with certainty on autopsy.

The brain of a person with Alzheimer's shows significant deterioration of tissue in the hippocampus and the frontal and temporal lobes of the cortex. There seems to be a build-up of protein "plaques and tangles" on neurons, particularly those with acetylcohline as the neurotransmitter (other transmitters such as norepinephrine, serotonin and dopamine are also involved). Research has indicated there may be a genetic deficit on chromosome 21 that results in the protein build-up. Treatment would include nourishment, exercise, and possibly "smart drugs" such as piracetam, a psychoactive drug that often improves cognitive functioning.

Q: **Can Alzheimer's Disease be detected early in life (19)?**

A: Whether an individual suffers from Alzhemer's or plain old senile dementia can only be determined with certainty in an autopsy. The brain of a person with Alzheimer's will show marked deterioration in the folds of the cortex... it looks like the brain has shrunk, and in a very real sense, it has. There is also a build up of amyloid protein, resulting in the actual destruction of neurons. The most consistent risk factor for Alzheimer's Disease is family history—researchers have reported genetic tags on chromosomes 1, 14, 19 and 21 (abnormalities associated with chromosome 21 can result in Down Syndrome, a disorder linked to amyloid plaques as well). However, about half of those who develop Alzheimer's Disease show no family history at all. Recently, the existence of a blood protein, ApoE, has been linked to Alzheimer's and potentially, this could be used as a screening test.

Q: **I've heard that aluminum may cause Alzheimer's Disease. Should I worry about drinking from aluminum cans (20)?**

A: Not at all. The major risk factors for Alzheimer's Disease are increasing age and family history. About 3% of North Americans between 65 and 74 years old have Alzheimer's. This figure rises to 20% for those between 75 and 84, and almost 50% for those over 85. Twin studies indicate that there is a substantial genetic component to the disorder. If one identical twin develops Alzheimer's, there is almost a 50% chance that the other twin will also develop it. Women have a slightly higher chance of acquiring the disorder and individuals with Down Syndrome will almost certainly develop Alzheimer's.

The link to aluminum comes from the observation that the neural "tangles" in the brains of Alzheimer's patients seem to contain a large amount of aluminum (there is a build up of a particular kind of protein -- so called "plaques and tangles--in the brain cells of people with Alzheimer's Disease). As a result, many people believe that use of aluminum cans and cookware might put you at risk. While one study shows a relation between aluminum consumption and Alzheimer's (Martyn, 1989, Lancet, 8629:59), most researchers believe that there is no convincing evidence of such a relationship.

Q: **Does stress help us to remember information (like phone numbers) or does it make us forget (21)?**

A: The effects of a stressor on memory will depend to a certain extent on how well learned the material is. For example, in a novel situation, high levels of stress and arousal can interfere with memory. This is typically the situation in eyewitness testimony. Imagine yourself as the victim of a robbery. It takes place very quickly, your attention is likely to be focused on targets other than the thief's face (e.g., you look at the gun he or she is holding), and the arousal may interfere with memory consolidation. Here, the stress works against your being able to recognize the individual accurately, because the dominant reaction is one that works against memory. However, we are likely to recall material that is well learned, e.g., emergency phone numbers (such as 911). The arousal once again results in a dominant response, but this time the response has been rehearsed and is likely to be remembered.

Q: **I was reading a chapter on memory that stated eyewitness testimony could be discredited due to memory construction. Is it also possible that along with memory construction, leading questions can also cause memory distortion? Also, if an event was a very emotional one for the witness, can this person's testimony be considered inaccurate due to "flash bulb" memories (22)?**

A: We tend to place a lot of weight on the testimony of an eyewitness. After all, that person was there and saw everything, right?

Well, maybe not. Elizabeth Loftus and others have shown that eyewitness testimony may not be as accurate as we think. The problem is that most eyewitness situations involve highly emotional activity (e.g., a robbery) and occur very quickly. Both of these factors contribute to poor, not enhanced memory. Furthermore, we do tend to reconstruct our memories. As we recall the event, we "fill in" any gaps, so that the memory we have for the event is quite complete. Leading questions most definitely influence recall. In one study, Loftus has demonstrated that more people agree with a leading question regarding an accident (e.g., "Did you see the stop sign?") compared to a less leading version (e.g., "Did you see a sign at the intersection?"). The emotionality of the situation interferes with memory rather than creating an accurate "flash bulb" type of memory.

Q: **If the proper cue could be found, would it be possible to retrieve any memory (23)?**

A: We do not lay down a permanent memory trace for every single thing with which we are presented. True, most material will enter the sensory register, but if we do not attend to it and process the information further, it is lost forever. Material that receives elaboration will most likely make it to long term storage, unless there is a disruption in the encoding process. For example, a very shocking event may occur (someone points a gun at you) and the memory trace does not become fully consolidated. Even for material that makes it to long term storage, we might forget it through decay over time, or perhaps through damage to certain parts of the brain. In all of the above cases, a retrieval cue will not help. In some cases, retrieval will be aided by an appropriate cue, but the memory trace first must be present.

Q: **Is any particular type of music related to memory recall in positive or negative ways? How and why (24)?**

A: As you may have noticed, advertisers frequently use music to help associate brands or products with a particular tune or jingle. Some studies in this area have produced positive results while other research studies show mixed or negative results.

Researcher Richard Yalch (1991) conducted two experiments that showed that music did enhance recall for brands or products. He found that items associated with musical jingles are easier to retrieve from memory but the pairing of items with music did not enhance recognition of those items. (Davis & Palladino, 1997).

In general, whether or not music has a positive or negative effect on your memory will depend on whether you heard the music when you were learning the material and the kind of mood it creates. If the music was present in the learning phase, it can act as a retrieval cue during recall (thus, improving memory). If the music changes your mood, then it may depend on whether the information you're concerned about has a positive or negative emotional tone to it. If it has a positive tone and the music makes you feel good, memory should be enhanced. Similarly, the information has a negative tone and the music makes you feel bad, memory will also be enhanced. Memory deficits show up when the feeling generated by the music does not match the emotional tone of the information. Gordon Bower refers to this as a mood congruity effect.

Developmental Psychology

One thing that we all share as humans is development. We mature, acquire cognitive and social skills, begin to speak, and integrate ourselves into a culture. While each of our cultures may be very different, it is fascinating that certain aspects of development are "universal"--all humans seem to have certain abilities that manifest themselves at about the same time. Consider smiling. All human infants will smile--even if they are blind at birth. Similarly, all infants respond to basic speech sounds (phonemes) in any language for the first 6-12 months of life. It is only after we have been exposed to a particular culture that we begin to respond only to that language. If you're thinking that it would be easier to learn multiple languages if you were exposed to them from birth, you'd be right!

Q: **What is a "critical period" (1)?**

A: The term "critical period" refers to a relatively narrow developmental window during which exposure to a particular environmental stimulus is essential for normal maturation in a species. For example, young ducklings will "imprint" on and follow the first moving object they see during the first 24 hours of life, whether it is the mother duck or a research scientist like Konrad Lorenz. The white-crowned sparrow must be exposed to the adult bird song sometime between the third and sixtieth day of life or it will never develop the song of its species.

A "critical period" may also refer to a time frame during which exposure to a particular environmental toxin can result in various birth deficits. For example, exposure to the drug Thalidomide during the first trimester of a pregnancy may result in the fetus being born with improperly formed limbs. Critical periods exist for many processes during development.

Q: **Recently, my AP Psychology class and I saw a video tape entitled "Secret of the Wild Child." This was a NOVA special featuring the unique story of the young girl who was found in California in the early 1970's after having endured almost total social isolation. The students and I were curious to know where and how Genie is today. Could you tell us what became of her (2)?**

A: The story of Genie is both interesting and tragic. As you know, Genie did acquire some language abilities, but her progress began to slow. Her vocabulary developed to about the level of the typical 3 or 4 year old, but no further. When the research project ended in the 1970s, Genie lived in a variety of foster homes. There was a report that she was harshly punished in one home (for vomiting) and from then on refused to speak. Shortly thereafter, she turned 18 and was made a ward of the state. The last thing I could find on her is that she now lives in a home for mentally retarded adults and does not speak at all.

Cases such as Genie's tell us much about the development of language and the need to have appropriate adult models in the environment.

Q: Young infants seem to show a preference for looking at faces. Could this be due to the fact that faces are the only things they've seen in the delivery room (3)?

A: At birth, infants will show a preference for looking at faces over other patterned objects. However, it is unlikely that this is due to the experience of viewing faces in the delivery room. First of all, infants are exposed to a great number of complex displays from birth, including faces (think of other objects in the delivery room). Moreover, this preference has been demonstrated as early as nine minutes after birth--hardly enough time to learn a complex discrimination task. Nonetheless, a facial pattern with the elements in the correct positions is the preferred display. This suggests an innate component for preferential looking.

Q: Can the smaller Y chromosome be considered genetically "inferior" to the larger X chromosome (4)?

A: In a way, yes. Humans have 23 pairs of chromosomes. Twenty-two of the pairs are called autosomes and are identical in length. The remaining pair are the sex chromosomes: XX in women and XY in males. The Y chromosome is actually shorter than the X by about half. This means that the Y chromosome has less genetic material than the X.

The most important implication of this discrepancy occurs when a recessive gene is present on the X chromosome, but finds no match on the Y. Ordinarily, we would match the two gene locations and only if both genes were recessive would the recessive trait be expressed. However, if a dominant gene on the Y does not counter the recessive gene on the X chromosome, then the trait would be expressed. This explains why males are more likely than females to have sex-linked disorders such as red-green color blindness.

Q: **If eye color is the result of a dominant (brown) allele and a recessive (blue) allele, how can you have green eyes? Using a Mendel table, the color should be either brown or blue, shouldn't it (5)?**

A: It would seem that it should be impossible to have any eye color other than brown or blue if we strictly apply Mendel's laws for the crossing of dominant and recessive alleles. After all, what are the possible combinations of two alleles that together code for either brown or blue eyes? But the situation is a bit more complex. Rather than two alleles determining eye color, there are actually three pairs of additive genes (six alleles) that code for color. This yields a dominance coding of 0 to 6 for eye color, and in humans, eye color can vary from a very light shade of blue, to completely black, with every shade in between (including green).

Q: **What is the likelihood that the genes for a mental disorder can be passed down from your parents? Would the home environment have any effect (6)?**

A: There is a lot of research on the heritability of various mental disorders, but the most extensive literature is on schizophrenia. Researchers have reported a definite genetic link. For example, Gottesman (1991) reports that your chance of developing schizophrenia is about 1% in the general population, but increases to 10% if a blood-related parent or sibling has the disorder, and 50% if both parents have the disorder.

You might argue that these data alone do not show a clear genetic link--and you would be right. It may well be the case that living with parents who have schizophrenia is very stressful and it is this exposure that results in the higher likelihood of developing the disorder. However, data from both adoption studies and twin studies confirm the original theory. Biological relatives of adopted children--children who later developed schizophrenia-- were four times more likely to have the disorder themselves as compared to the biological relatives of a control group of adoptees who did not have schizophrenia. For identical twins (who are 100% genetically similar), there is approximately a 50% concordance rate: If one twin develops schizophrenia, there is a 50% chance that the other twin will also develop the disorder. Concordance drops to about 20% for fraternal twins.

Thus, the available evidence points strongly to a genetic link for schizophrenia. Note, however, that there is plenty of room for environmental influence as well. The concordance rate for identical twins is only 50%. Thus, an individual may be genetically predisposed to develop schizophrenia, but this alone does not guarantee that the disorder will develop. Other factors (e.g., environmental) are likely to be involved.

Q: **I have a project for school and I need information on how nurture and/or nature affect sex roles a relationship. Where can I get information (7)?**

A: One place to start looking is in material relating to sociobiology. A number of authors have recently discussed the role of nature in a variety of situations including sex roles, the workplace, etc. Look for articles and books by E.O. Wilson or D.M.Buss. Check the article by Buss on Human Mate   Selection, American Scientist, 1985, vol. 73, p. 47-51. For an opposing view, see the book on sex roles by Alice Eagly, *Sex Differences in Social Behavior : A Social-Role Interpretation* (1987).

Q: **Are couples who have twins more likely to have twins again (8)?**

A: Twins and multiple births tend to run in families. So if you are a twin, you have a better chance of having twins yourself compared to a non-twin couple. However, a couple who gave birth to twins in the first place are not necessarily more likely to have twins during a second pregnancy. It depends on whether either member of the couple has a twin brother or sister.

Q: **Is it true that people with PKU can't drink milk (9)?**

A: Phenylketonuria (PKU) is a recessive, single gene disorder that affects about 1 in 10,000 people in North America.   The problem is the lack of a particular enzyme—phenylananine hydroxylase. This enzyme helps to convert phenylalanine to tyrosine.   Without the enzyme, there is a build up of phenylalanine in the body and a shortage of tyrosine.   This leads to a lower than normal level of dopamine (made from tyrosine), abnormal brain development, and retardation.

A screening test for PKU can be given at birth.   If the level of phenylalanine is abnormally high, the infant will be placed on a special diet.   Many foods contain phenylalanine and need to be avoided.

Perhaps most serious is milk and the infant must be given a whole milk substitute. This special diet will reduce the degree of mental retardation, but will not completely prevent it. Note: it is important that the diet be started within the first few weeks in order for it to be successful. Later in life, an individual with PKU should continue to reduce the amount of phenylalanine in their diet, although the restrictions are lessened at this point.

Q: If a mother smokes during pregnancy, are there any effects on the fetus (10)?

A: Yes, there can be. While the fetus does not form a tobacco dependency, it is likely that the fetus will be delivered premature or underweight. Both are risk factors-the baby will need some specialized care at birth. The problem is most likely due to a decrease in blood flow to the placenta as a result of smoking. I am not aware of a critical period for these effects, but there probably is one.

Q: What is Fetal Alcohol Syndrome (11)?

A: Fetal Alcohol Syndrome (FAS) is the result of a mother consuming a great deal of alcohol during pregnancy. Alcohol can penetrate the placenta and is transferred to the fetus. An FAS baby is likely to be born with a low birth weight, poor muscle tone, and will be mentally retarded and physically deformed.

There is some research indicating that even small amounts of alcohol during pregnancy can have an effect on the fetus. Thus, it is probably wise to avoid alcohol (and tobacco) when pregnant.

Q: Is alcoholism genetic (12)?

A: To a certain extent, the answer is yes. Studies conducted with relatives of people with alcoholism typically show that about 50% of the variability can be attributed to genetic factors. The exact mechanism however, remains a mystery.

Henri Begleiter, psychologist at the State University of New York-Brooklyn, reported that both alcoholic fathers and their sons show a particular deficit in their EEG (electroencephalograph) tracings. A specific genetic component called P3 seems to be missing. Since P3 is related to attention mechanisms, the genetic deficit may involve attention. However, keep in mind that only 50% of the variability is attributable to genetics; the other 50% to environmental factors. Interestingly, Kendler and associates (1994) demonstrated that the environmental portion is not due to shared factors-such as living in the same house. Researchers continue to explore these factors. Our response to living with an alcoholic is quite individual.

Q: If a child is born with a mental disorder, will there be fewer folds in his or her brain (13)?

A: No, this is not likely to be the case. The folds that we observe on an individual's cortical surface (the "convolutions") effectively increase the processing power of the brain. We can get more tissue into a confined area if we fold it up than if we try to force it in flat. (Try stuffing sheets of paper into a coffee cup—you can get many more sheets in if you crumple them up.) A mental disorder may result in brain damage, but that does not necessarily mean that the folds will be smoothed out. More commonly, a particular region of the brain will be destroyed or severely damaged.

There are certain disorders (e.g., Alzheimer's Disease) in which the brain tissue atrophies and dies. In this situation, you can see the loss of tissue and it does appear that there are far fewer folds on the cortical surface. But a childhood mental disorder in which there is brain damage is more likely to produce a loss of tissue or damage to a very specific area.

Q: Can children develop schizophrenia (14)?

A: Yes this is possible. Typically, the onset of schizophrenia is in the late teenage years, but it may begin as early as thirteen or fourteen. From a technical perspective, a child over the age of five may be described as having schizophrenia. The major symptoms of thought disorder (hallucinations and delusions) are rarely seen in young children, but parents and friends seem to realize that there may be a problem. Individuals who develop schizophrenia are often described as "different" when they were children.

On the other side of the life span, it also is rare to see schizophrenia develop after the age of about 45. An elderly person may suffer from some form of senile dementia (literally, an unraveling of the mind), but it would be highly unlikely that this is a schizophrenic disorder.

Q: Is the term "mentally retarded" still acceptable (15)?

A: The various terms used over the years to categorize those who score at the extremes on an IQ scale have shown a great deal of change. In general, anyone who scores in the extreme range is referred to as "exceptional." An individual with an IQ score of over 135 will be classified as "gifted," while those who score below 70 are classified as mentally retarded. It is important to realize that we are talking about a technical classification here -- this is the terminology used in assessment protocols such as DSM-IV. In nontechnical conversation, we are more likely to use the term "developmentally disabled" or "mentally challenged." While this might seem a question of semantics (or political correctness), you should think about the effects of labels and how they can change our perceptions of individuals.

Q: **Can repeated exposure to stress result in an autoimmune disease (16)?**

A: This is a distinct possibility. Several researchers have reported that certain types of autoimmune diseases (e.g., rheumatoid arthritis) appear to get worse when the patient is experiencing a period of high stress. Others have suggested that stress may be a factor in the development of AIDS, and it would appear that you can induce an autoimmune disease in the lab by exposing rats to a constant stressor. The link between an autoimmune disorder and stress makes a lot of sense. Stress does suppress the immune function in the body through the action of glucocorticoids (also known as cortisol). Cortisol has effects very similar to epinephrine, and seems to directly suppress the action of white blood cells.

Q: **Do young children have a conscience (17)?**

A: Let's first consider what it means to have a conscience. To be "conscious" implies an awareness of self--we realize that we are a distinct entity in the world, a thinking being. Young children (e.g., under 12 months) do seem to have this sense of self. This is demonstrated nicely by the so-called "rouge" test. Reddish facial make- up is applied to the nose of a child and then the child is allowed to look into a mirror. Children under 12 months will smile and stare at the image (they like to look at "other" faces). Older children (18-24 months) will look at the image and then touch their own nose. The older children realize that it is "self" in the mirror.

To have a conscience in the moral sense is another matter. We need that sense of self, but above this we must have the ability to understand right and wrong. We feel guilty about something because we realize that a "rule" has been broken and that we are responsible. At first, this means that we will simply get into trouble, but later the guilt results from violating our own personal norms for behavior. When does this happen?

It is difficult to put an exact time line on moral development, but most child development researchers would suggest that it begins around two or three years of age. Moral reasoning begins to resemble the adult pattern around seven years of age.

Q: **Who achieves the highest stage of moral reasoning-boys or girls (18)?**

A: Neither. The data indicate that there is no difference in the level of moral reasoning achieved by girls versus boys. In over 100 studies looking at a sex difference in moral reasoning, the vast majority (95 out of 107) found no difference at all. In the remaining studies, males showed a higher level in eight investigations, while females excelled in five. This is not to say that males and females reason in exactly the same way. Psychologist Carol Gilligan has argued that men tend to see morality as a matter of justice-a concept based on rational principles of fairness. Women, on the other hand, see morality more in terms of compassion and responsibility. While this difference in approach does seem to exist, it does not hamper either boys or girls in achieving a high level of moral reasoning.

Q: **What are the causes of various attachment styles? Is it the parent's behavior or the child's (19)?**

A: Many authors have noted that an infant's temperament seems to be fixed quite early. Some babies are quiet, while others are very reactive. Babies who are irritable at birth are still likely to be irritable at age 2, and those who are relaxed, remain relaxed. There is some evidence of difference in baseline heart rate between these two types of children. So perhaps it is the infant's behavior that produces a certain attachment style. The "high-strung" baby is difficult to handle, and remains so regardless of the parent's behavior. While it is difficult to discount this interpretation completely, many believe that the behavior of the primary caregiver is extremely important. Mary Ainsworth reports that mothers who were sensitive in responding to their children had infants who were classified as securely attached. If the child was ignored, attachment tended to be insecure. Ainsworth's data suggest that this occurs regardless of the child's temperment.

Q: **To what extent does the lack of infant attachment adversely influence adult behavior (20)?**

A: The concept of attachment would not be very useful if there were no effects in later life. The data with monkeys (e.g., the Harlow studies) indicate that infants who are raised in isolation develop a number of problems in later life. They are withdrawn and show little of the standard monkey social behavior. In humans, the data indicate that infants who are securely attached at age two, remain confident and independent at age five. They are well adjusted and have many friends. This pattern is maintained into early adolescence.

Looking at adult behavior, a few studies have looked at subjective reports of attachment style (i.e., the subjects did not participate in a "strange situation" test at age two, but answered some questions about how they remembered their attachment). The results indicated that subjects who were securely attached as infants were more likely to have satisfying romantic relationships and were more likely to be romantically involved with someone currently. So it would appear that there are consequences of attachment style that extend into adult life.

Q: **If attachment is strong and secure at an early age, what happens when you move out on your own? Do you have to replace this secure attachment (21)?**

A: The fact that you are securely attached does not mean that problems arise when you leave home and "sever" the attachment. Remember that the term "securely attached" comes from Ainsworth's work on the "strange situation." A child is brought into an observation room with the primary caregiver. The securely attached child will explore the room and play when mom is present, become upset when she leaves, particularly in the presence of a stranger, and will run to her when she returns. This style allows for the development of independence and exploration of the environment. It does not have to be "replaced" when you move out.

Both Ainsworth and Bowlby thought that attachment was crucial for adult development. The securely attached infant would become a well-adjusted adult, ready to handle the demands of relationships. In fact, there is some evidence that people who were securely attached as infants have longer-lasting, more fulfilling romantic relationships as adults.

Q: **What causes dyslexia (22)?**

A: Dyslexia is a learning disability in which words or numbers are perceived or written backwards. It affects roughly 5—10% of the population, and is up to 6 times more likely to occur with boys than with girls. What does this suggest (see the answer at the end of this chapter)?

We're not completely sure what causes dyslexia, but most authors now believe that it is not a visual/perceptual problem as originally thought. Recent work suggests a language difficulty and that it may be related to verbal memory. The problem seems to reflect trouble breaking down language into smaller units.

Q: **What is dysgraphia (23)?**

A: Dysgraphia ("faulty writing") is a disorder of written language expression, related to the reading disorder dyslexia. Individuals with dysgraphia exhibit inconsistencies in their writing style, such as unfinished words or letters, illegible writing, or multiple spelling errors. Someone with "phonological dysgraphia" will have difficulty writing phonetically. The problem seems to be that they cannot sound out words. Thus, they struggle with unfamiliar words; familiar material does not seem to be a problem. The opposite problem, referred to as "orthographic dysgraphia," is a visually-based problem. Individuals with this disability can sound out and write words (even unfamiliar ones), but they have real difficulty spelling and writing irregular words. For example, the word " calf" does not look the way it sounds. If we were to write "calf" phonetically, the spelling would probably be "caff."

Dysgraphia may be the result of brain damage and typically, phonological dysgraphia results from damage to areas of the temporal lobe. Orthographic dysgraphia is a parietal lobe problem.

Q: **What does Freud have to say about the development of homosexuality in men (24)?**

A: Recall that in the Freudian theory of personality, individuals progress through a series of psychosexual stages that require a successful resolution for "proper" personality development. Freud considered the Phallic Stage as central to this process. In the Phallic Stage, the male child is presented with, and resolves the Oedipal Complex and in doing so, identifies with his father. Failure to resolve the Oedipal complex results in fixation at the Phallic Stage and could be seen as the basis of homosexuality in a Freudian interpretation. So, is there any evidence that gay men fail to resolve this complex and become fixated at the phallic stage?

Not really. For example, there is no evidence that gay men identify more strongly with their mother than with their father, or that they have failed to resolve the Oedipal Complex. Gay men do recall having poorer relations with their father as compared to heterosexual men, but so do lesbians. Thus, there is no strong evidence supporting a Freudian interpretation of homosexuality.

Q: **Is there any evidence to suggest that homosexuality is due to "nature" (25)?**

A: Yes, there is. The "traditional" explanation for homosexuality involved parenting style and the home environment (e.g., the absence of a parent in the home, early sexual trauma such as rape, etc.). However, the data indicate that these factors are not related to the development of homosexuality. There does seems to be support for a genetic link. In roughly 50% of the cases where one member of an identical twin pair was gay, the brother was also gay. Similar results have been reported for women. Several researchers have suggested that a lack of androgens during pregnancy may result in same-sex sexual preference, and at least one study (LeVay, 1991) reports that a specific area in the hypothalamus was smaller in homosexual men compared to heterosexual men.

At this point the data do not conclusively support a nature explanation over one based on nurture. Like most topics in psychology, it is probably the result of an interaction between the two. Whatever the explanation, children seem to be aware of their sexual preference by the time they are 10 or 11 years old.

Q: **Dyslexia is up to 6 times more likely to occur with boys than with girls. What does this suggest (26)?**

A: The higher frequency of occurrence in boys might indicate a sex-linked disorder. Indeed, there is some evidence of a genetic component, as dyslexia tends to run in families. Dyslexia also can be acquired as the result of brain damage to the left temporal lobe.

Intelligence, Language, & Cognition

What does it mean to be intelligent? Is intelligence a single entity or a multitude of factors? Is it merely whatever my test measures? The topics presented in this chapter go together quite nicely. Intelligence seems to be related to language in many ways and to the ability to think and reason. But there are other considerations as well. For example, we may want to look at a person's ability to manage interpersonal relationships and read nonverbal cues. Clearly people who can get along with others are "smart". Questions often involve issues of how to measure intelligence, how we learn language, and some more controversial topics such as group differences in measured IQ.

Q: **Can you explain cognition in a manner that a child would understand (1)?**

A: Let me try. The word "cognition" comes from the Latin term "cognitio," which means "to know" or "to become acquainted with." Thus, the field of cognition is the study of knowledge. Webster's Dictionary adds that cognition is the "psychological result of perception, learning, and reasoning." So to understand what knowledge is from a psychological perspective, we need to look at how information is coded, processed, and remembered. Cognition is used to refer to the process of thinking, which involves all of the above, and is sometimes used to refer to a thought itself. Note that the focus in all of these examples is on internal mental processes-cognition in many ways is the study of how the mind thinks.

Q: **Is it true that playing music to a baby while it is still in the womb can increase the child's intelligence (2)?**

A: This issue has received a lot of attention since the original article on music and intelligence appeared in 1993. The study (Rauscher, Shaw and Ky), published in Nature, claimed that listening to Mozart resulted in a temporary increase of 8 or 9 points in adult spatial intelligence. Dubbed the "Mozart effect," this assertion immediately drew attention from researchers, educators, and state governments. After all, if listening to a particular kind of music increases intelligence, then we should encourage the use of this music as much as possible. There are several commercial programs that do suggest an expectant mother should play Mozart (in particular the Sonata for Two Pianos in D Major) to her unborn child.

Is there any support for this effect? Rauscher claims that there are numerous studies showing support for this theory (even in unborn rats). But a recent issue of Nature suggests otherwise. Two different research teams report that the effect is either minimal (about 1.4 points) or nonexistent. It seems that more research is necessary to determine if there is indeed an underlying mechanism that is producing this "Mozart effect." If listening to Mozart increases intelligence, how might this work, and does it fit with what we know about the human brain?

Q: **What is savant syndrome and what causes it (3)?**

A: Savant syndrome is a very rare disorder affecting about 10 percent of those diagnosed with autism (the incidence rate for autism is about 4.5 per 10,000 in the general population). The classic symptoms of autism in childhood include difficulty speaking or an inability to speak, a physical disability, and an IQ score in the lowest range. Males are three times more likely to be diagnosed as autistic than females. Savants demonstrate extraordinary skills in one particular area (e.g., music or calculations). For example, Leslie can play any piece of music on the piano after hearing it once, but has an IQ score in the 20's. In the film, "Rain Man," Dustin Hoffman played a savant with lightning-fast counting and calculating abilities. He could rapidly perform math operations in his head (including square roots), but could not calculate the correct change for a 60 cent purchase if given a dollar. What causes this syndrome? Many psychologists feel that the syndrome results from damage to the left hemisphere while the child was developing in the womb. Because of the damage, the right hemisphere (which is more specialized for math and music abilities) compensates. However, more research is needed to arrive at a definitive answer.

Q: **If Savants are so good at counting, why can't they make change for $1.00 (4)?**

A: It seems that we have a bit of a problem here: Savants can perform extremely rapid mathematical calculations, but cannot give the proper change for $1.00. How can you account for this? Think about it. If I ask you to give change for $1.00, you immediately code the problem as a mathematical function requiring subtraction (e.g., $1.00 minus 60 cents). Thus, to solve the problem, you simply have to translate the question (change) into a math algorithm (subtract). Savants cannot perform this translation so easily. However, if you asked them to perform the operation (100 - 60), they would have no difficulty. In essence, different skills are involved.

Q: **Is it possible to have a mild case of Savant Syndrome? Could this be what "gifted" really means (5)?**

A: The simple answer to this question is "no". In order to be diagnosed as having Savant Syndrome, you would need to be autistic as well. Extremely talented people (e.g., Beethoven) may appear to have qualities similar to savants, but it is extremely unlikely that the talent results from a similar cause (brain damage). To be classifies as "gifted" a child must demonstrate high performance in the arts, a scientific endeavour, or creativity. There is no particular cut off on an IQ scale, but most children classified as gifted would score in the top one or two percent on a standard test of IQ. This would translate to an IQ score of about 135.

Q: **What does a score of 90 on an IQ test mean (6)?**

A: Let's deal with this from a testing perspective first. Scores on a standard IQ test for adults (such as the Wechsler) will be distributed as a normal distribution with a mean of 100 and a standard deviation of 15. In other words, the average score on the test is 100. The standard deviation tells us about the spread of scores around the mean. Are they tightly clustered or do they spread out a lot? The higher the standard deviation, the greater the spread. In a normal (or bell-shaped) distribution, 68% of all the scores will fall within the window of +1.0 and -1.0 standard deviations from the mean. With the IQ test, 68% of all the scores fall within (100 + 15) and (100 -15), i.e., between 115 and 85. In fact, almost all of the scores (95%) will fall within + 2.0 or - 2.0 standard deviations--a range from 130 to 70. So, a score of 90 on an IQ test tells you that the individual scored 10 points or two-thirds of a standard deviation below the mean.

Does this mean that the individual is "less" intelligent? One must be careful in the interpretation of the numbers from an IQ test. Yes, the score indicates that the individual is below the mean, but whether or not this is really significant is questionable. To put this in perspective, consider that the designation of someone as "gifted" requires a score above 132; the designation as "retarded" requires a score below 70.

Q: **Is an I.Q. score of 186 valid? A psychologist advises us that 160 is the highest score for which an I.Q. test can test. And I read that a 50 year old who has the smarts of a 100 year old has an I.Q. of 200! The man in question may well be a "genius" - and I don't know what test was used or how old he was at the time. Hope you can help (7).**

A: The measurement of IQ has been a matter of debate for over 100 years. The validity of any particular number for IQ would depend on the scale used to measure it, and the age of the person taking the test. As you point out a 50 year-old who scores at the level of a 100 year old would have an IQ of 200. But this is not valid. First of all, the method use to calculate IQ (mental age divided by chronological age x 100) is the appropriate formula for use with the Stanford-Binet test. Norms for the test exist for children up to the early teens. After this point the Stanford-Binet test is not the appropriate one to use for testing IQ. Most adults will be given the WAIS-R, which is developed specifically for adults. The WAIS-R has some very nice statistical properties. The scale has a mean (average) of 100 and a standard deviation of 15 (this is a measure of variability). Using the WAIS-R, we would expect about 68% of the population to have a tested IQ between 85 and 115. Ninety-five percent of the population should score between 70 and 130, and 99.9% will score 40 and 160. The IQ score of 160, typically is listed as the highest score shown on the chart. Can you score higher? Yes, but it is extremely unlikely. Moreover, it probably does not really mean anything. To put the score in perspective, the standard cut-off to be considered "intellectually gifted" is an IQ of 135. So it looks like the advice you had is correct for intents and purposes.

Q: **If you administered both the Stanford-Binet test and the WISC test to the same person would you get the same IQ score (8)?**

A: Not necessarily. Even though I.Q. would be calculated using the same method (deviation IQ), the two tests have different subscales, different items, and different norms. Thus, similar performance on the two tests could result in a different estimate of IQ. This is especially problematic as we move away from the mean of the distribution. Extremely high (e.g., an IQ of 160 or more) or extremely low (e.g., less than 30) scores could be quite different on the two scales—perhaps as much as 30 points. Mensa recognizes the scale difference by publishing different required IQ scores for membership: 132 on the Stanford-Binet or 130 on the WISC.

Q: **What is the distinction between Thurstone's theory of intelligence and that offered by Sternberg (9)?**

A: These two theories of intelligence have a lot in common. Both are multiplex theories—they suggest that intelligence is more than a single quality. This is in direct contrast to people like Galton or Spearman who suggest that intelligence is unitary; a single factor like general intelligence ("g") or reaction time. Thurstone believed that intelligence was best thought of as a collection of **primary mental abilities**—skill sets in different areas of expertise that were more or less independent (e.g., math and vocabulary). Thurstone identified 7 primary mental abilities using his version of a statistical program known as factor analysis. Other people have suggested many more abilities, but in each case they would be viewed as unrelated. Sternberg's theory suggests that there are qualitatively different ways of expressing intelligent behavior. Some of these ways are covered by traditional measures, but others reflect a person's ability to survive in day-to-day situations. Moreover, Sternberg's theory is hierarchical—there are subgroups for each of the three major categories of intelligence. As such, the types of intelligence within each of the major categories are not unrelated.

Q: **What is the distinction between fluid and crystallized intelligence (10)?**

A: This notion of intelligence was proposed by Raymond Cattell in 1971. It is a hierarchical model and suggests that general intelligence ("g") is really composed of two subtypes of intelligence. Fluid

intelligence reflects an individual's "raw abilities"
such as inductive reasoning and logical thinking.
Crystallized intelligence is your own personal
knowledge base on a variety of topics such as
vocabulary and factual information. Cattell's
approach provides a compromise between a
unitary model of intelligence (e.g., Spearman's "g")
and a mutiplex model (e.g., Thurstone's primary
abilities). Interestingly, fluid intelligence may decline
with age, but crystallized often increases over the
course of one's life.

Q: **Can your IQ level change over time (11)?**

A: The answer to this question depends on your
definition of IQ. The term, "Intelligence Quotient"
was coined, not by Binet, but rather by Terman.
Terman adapted the Binet scale for use in the
United States while he was at Stanford (thus, we
have the Stanford-Binet scale). Terman extended
Binet's concept of mental age, by defining the
Intelligence Quotient as (mental age divided by
chronological age) x 100. Thus, the concept of IQ
was introduced. An IQ score of 100 means that you
are performing at the level one would expect for
your actual chronological age. You should note that
this IQ scale is intended for use with children only.
The norms are established only for children, and
the calculations become "strange" for adults. For
example, if a 50-year-old adult performed at the
level of the average 100-year-old, the calculated IQ
would be 200!

But what exactly is intelligence? Cattell suggests
that we look at two distinct types: Fluid (reflecting
mental processing ability) and crystallized
(reflecting our experience and knowledge of the
world). Typically, fluid intelligence decreases once
we are past the mid-teens, but crystallized remains

fairly constant and may increase across the life span.

Q: **In one question, you note that the Stanford-Binet test uses the concept of Mental Age to measure I.Q., but, in fact, the Stanford-Binet uses a deviation I.Q. score. Comments (12)?**

A: You are correct in pointing out that the Stanford-Binet scale has switched (quite some time ago) to using deviation IQ scores rather than the older concept of mental age/chronological age. However, most texts continue to refer to the use of mental age, primarily for a historical prospective. While the deviation IQ scores provide a more accurate measure, most investigators prefer to use some version the WAIS when assessing adult intelligence. The items on the WAIS are more appropriate for adults than the Stanford-Binet items, which is useful up until 16 or 17 years of age.

Q: **What is the "Chitterling Test" (13)?**

A: The issue of whether or not intelligence tests are biased is demonstrated nicely in the "Chitterling Test" developed by Adrian Dove in 1968. Dove (and others) have argued that the answers to standard intelligence test questions are culturally biased. Whether or not you know the answer depends not so much on your IQ as it does on the language and customs you are used to. The Chitterling test asks for knowledge-based information that would only be familiar to members of certain parts of North America (e.g., "How long do you have to boil chitterlings before they are ready to eat?"). If you are not familiar with chitterlings, you will have difficulty answering the question, just like some people may have difficulty answering other knowledge-based questions. In case you're wondering about the answer, we supply the following recipe from "The Joy of Cooking".

"Just after slaughtering, empty the intestines of a young pig while still warm by turning them inside out and scraping the mucous covering off completely. Wash in cold water then soak for 24 hours, refrigerated in cold, salted water. Wash again five or six times. Remove excess fat, but leave some for flavor. Boil for three to four hours."

Q: **Are there really racial differences in intelligence (14)?**

A: This is a hotly debated topic. Several authors have claimed that there are (e.g., Jensen, 1969; Herrnstein & Murray, 1994), while others maintain that any observed differences are due to other factors (e.g., Gould, 1995; Sternberg, 1995). So what's the real answer?

Let's begin by looking at the data. In many published articles, it has been reported that there is a difference in the measured IQ of blacks and whites, with whites scoring about 1 standard deviation higher. Most researchers accept this as "accurate". The real question is not whether there is a difference (there is), but rather what is it due to.

Jensen and others have argued that the difference stems from genetics. Critics point out that there are too many variables to say clearly. For example, there are strong environmental factors in the average living conditions of blacks and whites. It is also possible that the tests may be biased or fail to examine all the components of intelligence. Furthermore, any arguments based on heritability are likely to be in error. Heritability assesses factors due to differences within a particular group, not between groups. Thus, if intelligence can be shown to be due to genetic factors within a particular group, this does not mean that genetic factors are the cause of differences between groups.

The debate on this issue is likely to continue. The ultimate answer will have to be grounded on proper scientific investigation with an examination of all relevant factors.

Q: **What is emotional intelligence? Is it the same thing as IQ (15)?**

A: Emotional Intelligence is a concept proposed by Salovey and Mayer in 1990.

They suggested that there were a number of abilities that were related to intelligent behavior, but were not tapped by standard measures of IQ. These abilities all relate to the emotional and interpersonal side of our lives rather than the internal cognitive dimension. For example, Mayer and Salovey (1997) have defined emotional intelligence as

"the ability to perceive accurately, appraise, and express emotion; the ability to access and/or generate feelings when they facilitate thought; the ability to understand emotion and emotional knowledge and the ability to regulate emotions to promote emotional and intellectual growth."

Note: even though the term "emotional I.Q." is used, this is not a standard Intelligence Quotient that you find on a Stanford-Binet test. Mayer, DiPaulo, and Salovey (1990) have published an abilities test for emotional intelligence in the Journal of Personality Assessment, Volume 54, page 772.

Q: **Is it common for autistic children to have one "outstanding" ability (16)?**

A: No it is not. In fact, the display of an "outstanding" ability is quite rare. Autism (often referred to as childhood autism) is a puzzling disorder afflicting about 6.5 children in every 10,000 in North America. It is much more frequent in boys than in girls and is usually identified before a child is 30 months of age. Autistic children seem to have little need for social interaction or affection (even from their parents). They are withdrawn and appear isolated and within themselves. There is a marked lack of speech, or extremely limited talking-they will repeat exactly what someone else has said. There may also be prolonged, repetitive movements such as rocking or head banging. The vast majority of autistic children (about 80%) show intellectual problems severe enough to classify them as mentally retarded.

Only a small proportion (about 10%) will demonstrate an "outstanding" ability, e.g., being able to perform lightening-fast mathematical calculations (Dustin Hoffman portrayed such a "savant" in the film, Rain Man). Psychologists are not really sure what causes autism, but the data suggest a genetic deficit or some kind of damage to the genes during development.

Q: **Is "Motherese" universal -- does this appear in all cultures (17)?**

A: "Motherese" is readily observed when an adult interacts with a baby. We seem to have a tendency to speak in a high-pitched voice with exaggerated intonation and emphasis. One theory concerning this speech pattern is that it facilitates language acquisition by providing a very clear, easily

understood version of language for the new
speaker. There is a certain amount of support for
this view. Babies prefer this type of speech to
normal adult language. But it is not universal.
Motherese is encountered in most Western cultures
where the child is viewed as distinctly different from
the adult. In other cultures, the child is seen as
more "adult-like" from birth -- an individual who
needs no special language. They find the antics of
Westerners with their children quite laughable.

Q: **I'm really confused when it comes to figuring
out how many morphemes there are in a word.
Is there a simple way (18)?**

A: A morpheme is the smallest component of a
language that has meaning (as compared to a
phoneme, which is the smallest discrete unit of
sound in a language). When added to a root word,
a morpheme will change that word into another part
of speech, or alter the root by making it plural,
negative, etc.

Consider the word "dispassionately". How many
morphemes are present? Let's start by determining
the root word. In this case, the root is "passion"--
this is the first morpheme. Note that I cannot break
the root word into smaller units and still keep the
context intact. "Passion" refers to having an
emotional involvement in some activity or topic. I
could break the word into two parts: "pass" and
"ion". Both of these are words, but neither relates
to the overall concept and each has a meaning of
its own.

So the root is the noun, "passion". The suffix, "ate",
turns the noun into an adjective (morpheme
number 2), the suffix, "ly" turns the adjective into an
adverb (morpheme number 3), and the prefix, "dis"

turns the adverb into a negative form (morpheme number 4). Thus, we have 4 morphemes in the word "dispassionately).

Q: What's the first word that an infant learns (19)?

A: An infant will begin to speak when they are between 10 to 20 months old. The early vocabulary is quite simple, and contains basic nouns (e.g., "mama"), adjectives (e.g., "hot") and interactions (e.g., "hi"). But the word that seems to be the most frequently used at this time is "no". Whether or not this is the first word learned is difficult to say, but it would make some sense.

Q: What is the longest word in the English language (20)?

A: A good, unabridged dictionary will contain 250,000 to 300,000 entries. The average student will have a vocabulary of about 150,000 words by the time she or he finishes university. We really do not need all of those words to communicate. Just about anything in English can be said with a vocabulary of 850 words, and most of those words are quite "short" -- the correlation between word frequency and word length is -0.75.

So, what is the longest word?

Many people would predict that it is antidisestablishmentarianism, but no, this 28 letter word is eclipsed by the 45 letter word for a lung disorder:

pneumonoultramicroscopicsilicovolcanoconiosis.

Personality

Are people more as less "predictable"? Do they have stable traits and characteristics or does their behavior change with each situation they find themselves in? These are not easy questions to answer, but it's probably a little of both. There are some characteristics of personality that seem to be more or less fixed, while others aspects are malleable and can depend on the situation. A popular source for questions in this chapter is Freud's psychodynamic theory. It is here that we encounter and try to understand the Id, Ego, and Superego. Dream symbols and defense mechanisms generate a lot of discussion.

Q: **Is it true that Freud was addicted to cocaine (1)?**

A: No, there is no evidence that he was addicted. Freud used cocaine for about ten years, mostly while he was in medical school at the University of Vienna and later while he was an intern at Vienna's general hospital (the period from about 1873 – 1883). From the early days, Freud was interested in neurophysiology and the central nervous system. He actually discovered the anaesthetic properties of cocaine, but it was an associate of Freud's, Carl Koller, who pursued the idea and received credit for the finding. Freud was, however, quite dependent on tobacco. His passion for cigars eventually killed him—he died from mouth cancer in 1939.

Q: **Are dreams and visions something to worry about? Do they affect our lives in any way (2)?**

A: To answer this question, let's first consider what a dream really is. From the Freudian perspective, a dream represents the unconscious desires of the Id. These desires are pretty basic (food, sex, shelter), and the Id really "needs" to have these desires expressed. Other parts of our personality (e.g., the Ego) find these desires unacceptable for public expression and censor them in our day-to-day lives. Freud argued that these urges are expressed in our dreams-they are still censored (urges are represented by various symbols), but are allowed out in this "theatre of the night.

A very different view is expressed in the Activation-Synthesis hypothesis (Hobson & McCarley, 1977). According to this theory, dreams are nothing more than our interpretation of neural activity generated by a structure in the brain called the Pons. Various areas of the brain responsible for memory and sensation are stimulated or activated, and because these neural circuits are active, the cortex tries to make sense of the activity by synthesizing the information. This somewhat incoherent editing of neural activity is what we call a dream.

If you follow the Freudian approach, dreams can have meaning. They would reflect our unconscious urges and desires. From the activation-synthesis perspective, dreams are virtually meaningless. They are a reflection of the cortex trying to make sense out of "random" neural activity. Most researchers would agree with the activation-synthesis approach. Dreams do seem to be our way of interpreting internal neural signals. We do this in a way that is highly personal-with our own memories and sensory experiences. So dreams are not something to worry about. But if you are concerned (e.g., they may be disrupting your sleep), you should talk to your family doctor.

Q: **If you dream that you are falling and if you hit the ground, will you die (3)?**

A: The belief that dreams are predictive of the future leads us to think that dreaming of death results in death. But once again, there is no evidence to support this claim. People have recalled dreams where they fell and actually hit the ground. Most of the time, the dream does not end this way because we tend to wake up before we hit -- a lot of arousal is generated. Perhaps this leads us to the mistaken conclusion that there is some line in a dream that can not be crossed (e.g., hitting the ground). But no, dreams are unbounded... we can cross the line.

Q: **Is it true that when you have a dream that is in color that you are at the happiest point in your life (4)?**

A: No, it is not the case that full color dreams are related to any particular period in your life. In fact, most dreams are in color, not black and white. So why might we believe that there is some relationship? Dreams are very fleeting images. When we wake up, the memory is gone in a matter of seconds. We tend to remember the vague content of the dream before it fades, but very little about the "production values". We tend to think of dreams as black and white simply because we do not recall the color. The more vivid and dramatic a dream, the more likely we are to remember it. So it may well be the case that when we recall a full color dream, we do remember something very happy. Note that we may just as easily recall a full color nightmare too.

Q: **How do you figure out that a particular symbol stands for something else in a dream (5)?**

A: The notion that dreams are more than they appear to be is an important aspect of many psychodynamic theories. Freud called dreams the "Royal road to the unconscious" -- he believed that one could examine the content of dreams in an effort to tap urges and desires that had been hidden form the conscious mind. We are driven by the dark, unconscious part of our personality (the Id), but the Ego keeps these urges from being expressed -- even in our dreams. Thus, dreams are disguised through symbolism. A particular object (e.g., a pencil) has been substituted for the real, underlying image (e.g., a penis). In Freud's terms, the latent content has been disguised by the manifest content.

But how do we know what the pencil "stands for"? Is the pencil really a symbol for a penis or does it represent some other image, e.g., a finger? Well we really don't know. The interpretation of symbols is driven by theory without a whole lot of empirical support. Freud felt that urges expressed by the Id were universal -- everyone in every culture would have a common set of urges as a result of being human. If so, then the symbols themselves must be pretty consistent (perhaps with a bit of variation). Another theory, however, may suggest a completely different set of meanings for any given image.

Q: **I read an article recently where they said that having a "wet dream" was a normal experience and did not reflect a psychological disorder. Is this true or does it really reflect a disorder (6)?**

A: The article you read is quite correct... "wet dreams" are the result of a normal physiological mechanism and do not reflect a psychological disorder. To understand this process we need to consider what a dream actually is. The Freudian or psychoanalytical approach would talk about unconscious, repressed desires. Dreams are a place where such desires can be expressed more freely, and the symbolism would be useful in understanding the urges of a particular individual.

There is little scientific support for the strict Freudian interpretation of dreams. Most psychologists (e.g., Hobson, 1995) would explain dreams as a result of the brain interpreting internal activity during sleep. During sleep, there actually is a lot of activity going on in various areas of the brain. In our conscious, waking state this activity would be interpreted in a manner consistent with sensory input and perceptual mechanisms. However, when asleep, we need to rely on internal processing entirely--we are unconscious and cannot use external sensory information (although we may be able to incorporate external events into our dreams). Thus, a dream is an interpretation of neural activity offered by the brain.

So how can we explain a wet dream? Wet dreams may be experienced by adolescent males. In the early teenage years, there are a number of hormonal changes occurring in the body. In addition, both social and sexual interaction becomes very important in the adolescent's life. Thus, it is not surprising that erotic themes may be used in the interpretation of brain activity. We know that REM sleep is associated with heightened heart rate, increased respiration, erotic dreams, and, for males, erection. This may result in ejaculation. Wet dreams will tend to disappear with age as sleep patterns change and other themes become important in one's daily life.

Q: **I got into a discussion with my psychology teacher today on the subject of defense mechanisms. He said, "a student blaming their poor grade on a 'hard' test" is an example of a defense mechanism. I raised a counter point: Doesn't his remark reflect his own defense mechanisms? By suggesting that the students did not study, isn't that a defense on the part of the teacher (7)?**

A: Absolutely, the type of behavior that you mention could be considered as a defense mechanism. Freud considered that such mechanisms were available to the Ego whenever repression was incomplete, or required too much energy. Ego could resort to such things as projection, reaction formation, etc. in an effort to keep Id's urges out of conscious awareness. Thus, to consider your professor's statement as a defense mechanism, we would have to assume that the idea of admitting to a bad exam is threatening for the professor, so he rationalizes by "blaming" the students. Similarly, we would assume that the idea of poor performance is threatening to the students, and they rationalize by blaming the professor. Note that we are not concerned with the actual state of affairs (i.e., whether it really was the student's fault or the professor's), only the justification provided by the Ego.

Q: **In the Freudian structure of the mind, is it fair to say that the Id is "selfish," and that the superego is "good" (8)?**

A: According to Freud, the Id represents basic human motivations, such as hunger, thirst, sex, etc. The Id functions in the unconscious mind and obeys the pleasure principle (maximize pleasure and minimize pain at almost any cost). Thus, we might consider the Id as "selfish" in that it is totally self-centered and simply wants desires fulfilled. To meet the demands of reality, the Ego develops and tries its best to satisfy the Id, given the constraints of everyday existence. The Ego does not worry about morality -- it simply operates to keep the Id in check. Morality is the domain of the Superego, a structure that rewards the Ego with praise for doing the right thing, and punishes with guilt for making the wrong decision. The Superego is definitely the moral authority, but that does not imply that the Superego is "good". Descriptions such as "good" or "bad", "right" or "wrong" are value judgments that depend upon whose system of values we are using at the time.

Q: **What's a Freudian Slip (9)?**

A: According to Freud, every thought and every behavior is motivated. All human action is the result of the urges of the Id, censored and evaluated by the Ego and Superego. Thus, you do not "forget" to mail a letter--you did not want to in the first place. We can come up with an explanation for our behavior, but it is a construction of the Ego, an attempt to satisfy the Id and repress the urge if necessary.

At times, the Ego has difficulty repressing the desires of the ID. On these occasions, the real urge will leak out and pass through the defenses set up by the Ego. This is a Freudian Slip. Note that on the surface, the slip appears to be an error in speech or behavior, often humorous. But according to Freud, this is the real urge being displayed.

For example, a colleague of mine once referred to "the behavior of orgasms", rather than "organisms". Freud most definitely would have something to say about this!

Q: **Why do we still talk about Freud (10)?**

A: The ideas of Sigmund Freud seem to have found there way into issues ranging from psychology to art to literature, and more. Something about what he had to say seems to touch a wide variety of interests. Perhaps the reason is that Freud gave us the notion of the unconscious and made us consider that there is a "dark" side to human existence, one that we might never really know about because it is out of our awareness.

Q: **Is it possible to switch between being a Type A versus a Type B personality (11)?**

A: Not really, but the scale itself may not be as stable and valid as was once thought. The original personality scale was developed by Friedman and Rosenman in the 1970's. Both were heart specialists and had noticed people who tended to develop heart problems tended to have a similar personality. They were the hard-driven "workaholic" type who never seemed to slow down. Friedman and Rosenman developed a personality scale to measure an individual's likelihood of developing coronary heart disease based on their profile. Those who were aggressive, competitive, easily frustrated, impatient, etc. were labeled **Type A's**. Those who lacked these symptoms were **Type B's**. Friedman and Rosenman demonstrated that Type A's were twice as likely to develop heart problems compared to Type B's. However, more recent research indicates that the hard-working lifestyle by itself is not so problematic. The real culprit is the intense irritability and aggression—these factors have repeatedly been associated with an increased risk for coronary heart disease. So, some of the behaviors we think of as "Type A" (such as showing up at the airport an hour early to make sure you do not miss the plane), may not be related to the profile at all.

Q: **What are ink blots made out of and how are they made (12)?**

A: There is no secret to ink blots--they're made by putting a blob of ink on some cardboard and folding it in half (at least the originals were made in this way). Modern printing procedures would probably use computer-generated images. The series used for projective tests (such as the Rorschach) have been specifically selected and are copyrighted.

Q: **What is Factor Analysis? I'm lost (13)!**

A: Factor analysis is a statistical technique that takes a large volume of data (e.g., questions on a personality inventory) and reduces it to a small number of "underlying dimensions" (i.e., the factors). These dimensions are determined by how strongly the various questions are associated with each other. Items that are "naturally" associated with each other should "load" or show up on the same factors, while those that are not associated should load on completely different factors.

For example, let's say that I ask 100 people to tell me their height, weight, annual income, level of education, and the number of cups of coffee they drink each day. We would expect that height should be strongly associated with weight because, in general, taller people are also heavier. Similarly, we would expect that annual income would be associated with level of education, but not with height and weight. Coffee consumption would probably not be strongly associated with any of the items.

If I ran a factor analysis on these data, I should expect that height and weight will load strongly on one factor with the other items showing very low factor loadings. However, on another factor, income and education should load strongly while height, weight, and coffee have very low loadings. Coffee consumption might produce a third factor where it loads strongly, but the other four items do not.

Ideally, the results of such a factor analysis should look like this:

Item	Factor 1	Factor 2	Factor 3
Height	1.0	0.0	0.0
Weight	1.0	0.0	0.0
Income	0.0	1.0	0.0
Education	0.0	1.0	0.0
Coffee	0.0	0.0	1.0

Looking at these results (the numbers can be thought of as correlation coefficients), I might label

Factor 1, **Body Size** (since physical dimensions seem to be involved), Factor 2, **Economic Level** (indeed, these items typically load on a factor called Socioeconomic Status), and Factor 3, **Caffeine Addiction**. Note that the labels are completely arbitrary--you might choose three entirely different names, e.g., Mass, Wealth, and Stress (since people under stress drink more coffee). Thus, the final labelling and interpretation of a factor analysis is open to discussion.

Q: **Where can I find various personality inventories on the web (14)?**

A: There are numerous sites on the web that have a variety of personality tests. Some of these are genuine, while others are more for "fun". Before you use any test from the web, be sure to check with the original author(s). In some cases, the test will have been altered and you will want to know which items have been changed. It is possible also that the particular test you are interested in is copyrighted and legally available only from the author and his or her agent. There may be a fee involved for the use of the test. To see some examples of materials available on the web, go to

www.vanguard.edu/psychology/webtesting.html

Most tests have been published in the journal, *Psychological Assessment* (see description at www.apa.org/journals/pas.html).

Q: **Where can I get some information about theories of personality (15)?**

A: Check out the following websites for a wealth of information.

www.learner.org/exhibits/personality/resources.html

This site is sponsored by the Annenberg/CPB Multimedia group

The "The Personality Project" Web site at pmc.psych.nwu.edu/personality.html

This site contains a rather large set of references to current papers and research in personality theory. The readings are organized by the approach taken to personality, so it may help with the theories of personality covered in introductory psychology. The site also has links to those papers that are online which greatly enhances access.

Q: **Can a personality test ever be "wrong" (16)?**

A: The answer to this question is "yes," but let's consider an important assumption behind the question: Is a personality test "right" in some real way? Personality tests such as the MMPI or the TAT are not objective taps on some underlying dimension of your psychological make-up. The tests are designed to present profiles that may be a more or less accurate index of personality.

For example, one popular personality test is Cattell's 16-PF. This test contains 16 subscales (or "factors") and each subscale has a number of statements for you to agree or disagree with. One of the subscales measures your degree of shyness. We might expect someone who is shy to disagree with the statement: "I like to attend parties as frequently as possible." If you responded to a number of statements in this fashion, you would end up with a high score on the shyness scale, and the personality test would "type" you as a shy person. You would fit the profile of a shy person.

Does this mean you really are shy? Maybe. It depends on a number of factors, including how well the scale distinguishes between shy and outgoing people, how well the statements tap the construct of "shyness," and how honestly you responded to the statements in the first place. So the test can be "wrong" because there are many factors that influence its ability to assess personality.

Social Psychology

Why do people do the things that they do? How do other people influence our behavior? What makes people fight? These questions are the domain of social psychology. Here we examine how the real or imagined presence of others influences our own thoughts and behavior. In many ways the study of social psychology is at the other end of the spectrum from biopsychology. Here we are interested in the broad picture—how we relate to other people and groups. At times, it may appear that we have entered the realm of sociology rather than psychology. In fact, you will often find a course called "social psychology" offered in both a psychology and sociology program. The topic of television violence and aggression tends to draw the greatest number of questions. Several of these are printed below.

Q: **Do we find a potential mate attractive because we are thinking (unconsciously) about how attractive our children might be (1)?**

A: No. I am not aware of any support in the research for this notion. However, certain theories might indeed predict this kind of mate selection. For example, sociobiologists might argue that perceived attractiveness should be linked to an individual's ability to have and raise children. People who have physical attributes most suited to child bearing should be seen as more attractive than those who do not have these qualities.

While appealing, this approach does not necessarily explain radical shifts in perceived attractiveness within a culture (e.g., the popularity of the ultra-thin look for women). It also does not address perceived attractiveness in homosexual couples.

Q: **Attractiveness is an important factor in changing attitudes. So how do you explain "social marketing"—ads that try to get you to contribute to various causes? The people in these ads are not necessarily attractive (2)**

A: There are two important factors to keep in mind here. First, the "attractiveness" in question is that of the communicator (the person making the argument), not the various people in the ad itself. Furthermore, we are not constrained to a consideration of physical attractiveness only. There are other qualities that may contribute to a communicator's overall level of attractiveness. Second, there are other avenues to persuasion. In this case, the appeal is not so much based on attractiveness as it is on emotion. The goal is to arouse sympathy. As such, the ad works through message factors rather than the attractiveness of the communicator.

Q: **I've often heard that "opposites attract." Is this true? Are people who are opposite in physical attractiveness likely to get along (3)?**

A: People are attracted to one another for a whole variety of reasons. Sometimes it is because we have the opportunity to interact, sometimes because we have similar interests, etc. One factor that consistently surfaces as very important in studies of dating couples is physical attractiveness. Quite simply, we like those who are attractive. But do we choose the most attractive people to date, and is the relationship likely to last if there is a "mismatch" in attractiveness?

The literature supports the Matching Hypothesis – people will choose to date someone who is about the same level of attractiveness as themselves. Moreover, the relationship is much more likely to last if both members of the couple are similar in physical attractiveness. This is partly due to the increased attention given to the more attractive member of a couple if there is a mismatch. Please note: physical attractiveness is not the only factor that people consider when choosing a date or a mate, and the importance of attractiveness will vary from person to person. Indeed, exactly what someone finds attractive is open to much interpretation. But the literature does indicate that, at least for dating, similarity, not complementarity, is the crucial factor.

Q: **Is the fundamental attribution error acquired through genetics or learning (4)?**

A: The fundamental attribution error (FAE) is the tendency to attribute dispositional or internal causes to other people's behavior. We tend to see others do things because of some trait-like characteristic, rather than some aspect of the situation. If we observe John trip over the curb, we tend to assume that John is clumsy, rather than the sidewalk might be broken. I should note that we have a bias to interpret our own behavior in the opposite way... if we trip over the curb, we attribute the action to an external source (broken sidewalk) rather than our own failings. So is this a learned bias, or are we born that way?

The FAE is almost assuredly learned. While one might argue that there is a certain degree of ego protection involved in making the FAE, it is not a universal phenomenon. For example, in cultures where the focus is more on the collective rather than the individual (e.g., in China), the FAE is not observed as strongly, if at all. In addition, individuals suffering from major depression will often reverse aspects of attributional bias to their own disadvantage. For example, they see success as due to external factors such as luck, while failures are attributed internally ("I'm just no good"). You might look for more information in the Journal of Cross Cultural Psychology.

Q: **I don't understand Cognitive Dissonance Theory. Can you help (5)?**

A: I'll do my best. Dissonance is a theory of attitude change first proposed by Leon Festinger in 1957. Festinger did not initially set out to come up with a theory of attitude change. Rather, he was trying to explain the psychological effect of earthquakes. Festinger noted that following a series of earthquakes in India, people who lived near the epicenter of the quake seemed to be quite calm. It was the people who lived furthest away who expressed the most fear. This did not make any sense—they were not in as much danger. Festinger reasoned that they must somehow be justifying their reactions, that is, things must be really bad if I'm afraid of it at this distance!

Festinger suggested that all of us have a need to be consistent. We do not like it when things are inconsistent, and we will try to regain consistency in whatever way we can. This need is the basic idea behind Cognitive Dissonance Theory. Festinger argued that we experience dissonance whenever there is some inconsistency between two of our thoughts (cognitions), or between an attitude and a behavior. For example, it would be inconsistent for me to believe that I am highly in favor of energy conservation and at the same time drive my big, gas-guzzling car to work. This inconsistency should generate that feeling of dissonance and motivate me to do something to reduce it. I could give up my car; justify my attitude by noting that lots of people drive big cars to work, or change my attitude. Festinger argued that in many cases, the easiest thing to do is to change the attitude. This is especially true when you can come up with little external justification for engaging in the behavior.

Let's look at the classic study by Festinger and Carlsmith (1959). Students were asked to lie about how interesting a really boring task actually was. The experimenter wanted them to tell others that the task was really quite interesting. They were offered either $1.00 or $20.00 to tell the lie. Everyone agreed to lie for the experimenter and then later they were asked how much they really liked the task. Think about it. In which condition would you say that you liked the boring task the most?

Dissonance theory predicts that the greatest change occurs in the $1.00 condition. If you ask yourself, "Why did I tell a lie?," you have a good answer in the $20.00 condition—the experimenter paid me a lot of money to do so. You can't come up with a good reason in the $1.00 condition. You told a lie and had no good external justification—this should cause dissonance. This is exactly what happened in the Festinger and Carlsmith study. Fortunately, you can reduce the dissonance by changing your attitude and justifying your behavior. You can conclude that the task really wasn't that bad after all.

Q: **Would a person, opposed to gambling because of his religion, feel a lot of dissonance if he gambles anyway and loses a lot of money (6)?**

A: At first he would, but the fact that the person continues to gamble suggests that he has resolved the dissonance by either changing his attitude (he is not really against gambling) or perhaps by reinterpreting the situation (e.g., he might believe that playing "proline" is not really a form of gambling). Thus, at this point in time, he is no longer engaging in counterattitudinal behavior—he is behaving in a manner consistent with his attitude and therefore there is no dissonance.

Q: **Why is timing important with the door-in-the-face technique (7)?**

A: Two standard compliance techniques are the foot-in-the-door (FITD) and door-in-the-face (DITF). To use FITD, the asker begins with a small request, and then follows with a larger one. In essence, you hook the customers by having them agree to a small request ("may I come in") and then hit them with the real pitch ("do you want to buy this vacuum"). Freedman and Fraser (1966) asked subjects whether they would agree to answer a few questions about household product use (small request), then a few days later asked if they would allow a team to come to their house to inventory all the products in their home (large request). Compliance with the large request doubled if subjects were first asked the small favor. Theoretically, FITD works because our self-image as a helpful person is established with the small favor, and we do not want to challenge this image when asked for the large request. DITF works through a different mechanism. Here we first make a large request that is likely to be rejected ("can

you lend me $50"), then follow it with a smaller offer
("O.K., can you lend me $5.00"). Bob Cialdini
suggests that the smaller request is more likely to
be granted (by almost a three to one margin) if the
large request is turned down first. But timing is
critical--the second request must quickly follow (not
so by the way for the FITD effect). This is because
the DITF effect is largely due to the pressure one
feels to reciprocate. The asker started high and
when you refused, they dropped their request to a
more reasonable second position. You feel
pressure to engage in a reciprocal concession of
our own and grant the second request.

Q: **If you change an attitude, how long will the
       change last (8)?**

A: It depends on how the attitude change was
       accomplished. Petty and Cacioppo (1985) have
       argued that there are two distinct routes to
       persuasion. The central route involves a careful,
       thoughtful consideration of the message. People
       who pay attention to message factors such as
       argument strength have a resulting attitude that is
       very strong and resilient. The peripheral route is a
       much less effortful way to persuade. Here we are
       influenced more by superficial factors such as
       communicator attractiveness. Attitudes changed in
       this fashion are not as strong and may be easily
       changed again. What determines whether we use
       the central or peripheral route? One important
       factor is issue involvement. If the topic under
       consideration will affect you personally, then you
       are more likely to engage in central processing. If it
       will not affect you, then peripheral cues seem to
       work best.

Q: Is catharsis a good thing or a bad thing? I've heard both (9).

A: Catharsis, a term introduced to psychology by Sigmund Freud, refers to the safe venting of desires such as aggression. Freud believed that human behavior was the product of unconscious drives such as the life force (eros) and the death force (thanatos). These darker drives had to find some release and catharsis provided a way to do this with the least harm and in a manner that was socially acceptable. For example, aggression might be safely vented by playing or even watching a contact sport. Is there any evidence in favor of the catharsis hypothesis?

Not really. While there are a few exceptions, most of the data indicate that watching aggression, for example, leads to increased not decreased aggression in the future. There may be a few short-term benefits, but the overall word on catharsis is that it does not work.

Q: Is TV violence getting worse (10)?

A: If we look strictly at the amount of programming that contains violence, the numbers have not changed very much over the past 30 years. Content analyses consistently show that roughly 80% of all programs in prime time contain some kind of violence. Children's programming (e.g., Saturday morning cartoons) actually is the "worst" offender with about 94% of the shows containing violence. And children do watch a lot of television— on average, about 30 hours a week. The intensity of the violent portrayals may have increased and the availability of "pay per view" channels may have increased violent offerings, but the overall pattern has remained much the same.

The real question is not so much how much violence is on TV, but rather, what are the effects of viewing violence?

Although there is some disagreement in the literature, the consistent finding is that viewing violence has a negative effect. The effect may not consist of direct imitation of some violent behavior, but is typically more subtle and results in disinhibition and desensitization to aggression. There are some very important qualifications to be made here; for example, the effect may be neutralized by one's ability to separate fantasy from reality. Nonetheless, we should be concerned about the level of violence in the media.

Q: **Regarding media effects and aggression, is "stylized" violence (such as the World Wrestling Federation) just as problematic (11)?**

A: One of the major factors determining whether media violence results in enhanced aggression is the viewer's ability to separate fantasy from reality. If the viewer believes that the media portrayal is "real" then, heightened aggression is likely to follow. However, when the viewer believes that the media image is purely fantasy, then increased aggression is far less likely. Leonard Eron has shown that a simple 3-hour training program in which children are shown how special effects are used to create violence is sufficient to prevent increased media-related aggression at a one-year follow-up! So, whether the WWF will increase aggression in viewers or not depends, in part, on whether one sees the WWF as real or fantasy.

Q: What about the effects of watching real violence on television, for example in the news? Are the results the same as with fictional acts of aggression (12)?

A: Watching violence can trigger violence in the viewer. When the violence is real (for example, a clip of a war scene on the nightly news), the effects can be the same as with fictional violence. In fact, you might argue that the effects should be more profound. First, the emotional reaction to the clip is likely to be more intense. After all, this is a real act of violence, and people are likely to feel anger, disgust, etc. To the extent that the clip produces a strong emotional response, you would predict from Excitation-Transfer theory that aggressive behavior is more likely with acts of actual violence.

Second, Leonard Eron, among others, has argued that a critical factor in determining whether or not filmed violence results in aggressive behavior is the viewer's ability to distinguish fantasy from reality. In essence, if you realize that the violence is faked, you will not be as likely to respond in an aggressive manner. News clips tend not to be faked--they represent actual acts of violence. Thus, we would once again predict a stronger aggressive response. It is important to remember that many factors may be operating here (for example, type of commentary, length of clip, etc.). Furthermore, TV violence leads to aggression only in those who are ready to aggress (e.g., those who are frustrated, angry, etc.). Violence on television does not automatically trigger aggression.

Q: When considering the effects of watching
      violence in the media, does the type of violence
      you watch matter? For example, I was
      depressed after watching *Saving Private Ryan*,
      but relatively excited after watching *The
      Matrix* (13).

A: While media violence effects are quite robust, it
      does indeed matter what type of violence you see.
      Perhaps the most important factor here deals with
      the perceived consequences of violent behavior. If
      the violence is portrayed as instrumental (you can
      get what you want), exciting, and as not having
      consequences for the perpetrators, the victims, or
      any of their friends and relatives, then we might
      expect relatively strong effects. Under these
      circumstances, we should predict that watching
      media violence would result in increased
      aggression in those individuals who have a reason
      to be aggressive (e.g., they are angry).

      However, if the violence is portrayed as senseless,
      with severe consequences, and anything but
      exciting, then we should expect little (if any)
      enhanced aggression after watching the violent
      behavior. Before we think that we have found the
      "solution" to media violence, we must remember
      that viewers will habituate and become
      desensitized to violence with continued
      presentations. It is quite likely that there would be
      no increased aggression following an initial viewing
      of Saving Private Ryan, but this may not be the
      case after watching the film for the fifth time. For
      more information about the major effects of seeing
      violence in the media, see the American
      Psychological Association's article, Violence on
      Television.

Q: **Does violence on TV make children do violent things? Do children get ideas from TV or do they think what they see on TV is real (14)?**

A: Television violence per se does not cause aggression. It does, however, make it more likely that aggression will occur in people who are predisposed to aggressive behaviors. In this way, it is a releaser—if the organism is ready to be aggressive, then TV violence can trigger the response. One important limiting condition is the degree to which people watching TV violence believe that the violence is "real" or fictional. If one believes that the violence is not real, then the show is less likely to produce more aggression. If, however, the viewers think that life matches what they see on television, then the violence can produce aggression. Thus the ability to distinguish fantasy from reality will, in part, determine whether or not TV violence influences aggression.

Q: **Did TV violence cause Columbine (15)?**

A: The suggestion has been made that TV violence (or violent video games) was, in fact, the cause of the Columbine shootings. There is an enormous amount of research on the effects of media violence. In general, the research indicates that media violence can influence subsequent aggression in those individuals predisposed to such behavior. What I'm suggesting here is that watching media violence may increase aggression, but only in the those individuals who are angry, frustrated, aroused, or have lowered inhibitions towards aggression in the first place. It is also important to remember that the effects of watching filmed violence are relatively short-lived. You may see increased aggression if it is measured relatively soon (e.g., within 30 minutes) after exposure to the media violence. This is not to say that there are no long-term effects—there are, e.g., desensitization to cues associated with violence, social learning, disinhibition and so on.

So, did TV violence cause Columbine? I don't think that it is quite that simple. Some form of media violence may have influenced Harris and Klebold. However, this would not have happened in a vacuum. Violent images may have desensitized the aggression and made it seem normal. But the images would not have generated the frustration or supplied the firepower used by Harris and Klebold. Media violence by itself is not the culprit.

Q: **It seems likely that media violence can influence aggression, but why are people "drawn" to media violence? Is this some kind of natural drive (16)?**

A: The issue of whether behavior is the result of nature or nurture is classic and still debated after many years. With simple types of behavior, it seems that the cause "must" be nature. After all, something like hunger does not seem amenable to environmental influence. Or is it?
While a basic drive like hunger is hard-wired, what we eat, when we eat, how we eat, etc. clearly can be affected by environmental input. So are people drawn to media violence?

Producers of violent programming often argue that people must want this type of material and that they are simply filling a public need. In reality, action footage is often used because it is relatively inexpensive. But are we drawn to it?

Not in the same way that a moth is drawn to a flame. We are not really talking about a biological imperative here. You could argue that attention is more likely to be directed to violent action footage, than to something more mundane. It is true that we pay more attention to salient stimuli (stimuli that are big, loud or colorful) as compared to more boring material, and that certain personality types prefer violent programming. But there are also those who abhor violence no matter how salient it is. Human behavior is very complex and not easily explained as the result of a single cause, no matter how compelling that cause might be.

Q: **What do people usually say when they are asked why they failed to help at an emergency situation (17)?**

A: Darley and Latane have noted that people will fail to intervene in emergency situations for a number of reasons. For example, they may not define the situation as an emergency, or they may believe that someone else should help. This is the classic unresponsive bystander effect. If you ask people why they failed to help, they will often rationalize along these lines. In one of the classic experiments by Darley and Latane, subjects filled out a questionnaire while smoke poured into the room from under a door. Subjects later offered reasons such as "they were sure the smoke did not reflect a fire" , or that it wasn't really smoke at all, but rather, smog or "truth gas" . In real emergencies, a similar result is found. Bystanders at the famous Kitty Genovese murder in 1964 in New York commented that they were sure someone else would have phoned about the incident, so they did not bother. In general, bystanders have to notice the situation, define it as an emergency, and assume responsibility before they even consider helping.

Q: **Is altruism related to religion, e.g., would a more religious person be less susceptible to bystander effects (18)?**

A: The data are not conclusive on this question. Some studies find higher levels of helping for very religious people, others find lower levels of helping. The higher levels of helping seem easily explainable, but how can you account for decreased helping?

Well it seems to depend on the underlying philosophy associated with the religion, particularly with respect to the question of responsibility for errors and mistakes. To the extent that people are seen as responsible for their behavior, we can see "victims" in this light as well. If they are responsible, then helping will decrease. I should note here that the seriousness of the victim's situation may overwhelm this effect.

Q: **Is the unresponsive bystander effect only found in North America (19)?**

A: The observation made by Darley and Latane regarding bystanders at emergency situations is fairly general across cultures. Recall that these authors found that the more bystanders were present at an emergency, the less likely it was that anyone would help. This counter-intuitive finding has been explained in a number of ways, but Darley and Latane favored two possibilities: social comparison and diffusion of responsibility. Different cultures may vary in how much importance they place on social comparison... the greater the emphasis, the more likely people will not want to make mistakes in public, and the greater the bystander effect.

Q: **During times of international conflict, does prejudice within a single country decrease (20)?**

A: Yes, we would certainly make this prediction. Muzafer Sherif studied intergroup conflict back in the 1950's and he noted that one of the best ways to reduce intergroup tensions was to establish a "superordinate" goal - a task that required the cooperation of both sides for their mutual benefit. This would appear to be the case with international conflict, at least within a single country. All groups are more united in the task of defeating the enemy. In addition, there is a cognitive recategorization taking place. War, in particular, casts the players into "us" versus "them", and as such, citizens of one country are all together in the struggle. Please note that other factors may come into play here. Prejudice should decline to the extent that previous nonaligned groups are now members of the same team. If these groups do not feel that they are equal partners in the new coalition, then prejudice may actually increase.

Q: **Are there any differences between individual and group decision making (21)?**

A: Indeed there are! Group or committee decisions are often worse than individual decisions. The quality of a group decision is influenced by many factors including:

The group's acceptance of common goals. The more group members accept the goals, the better the decision.

The status structure in the group. A high status member such as the leader may talk too much and his or her presence can influence what the group decides.

Group size. In general, small groups make better decisions than large groups.

Cohesiveness. The extent to which a group feels that it is a well-defined group (what Levin called a "we-feeling") will influence the quality of the group's discussion. High cohesion leads to greater participation and a decrease of tension. But, there may be a price to pay. Irving Janis described a process he called groupthink, a desire to reach a unanimous decision within the group that seems to override both common sense and individual members' better judgment. Janis suggested that many political disasters (such as the decision to invade Cuba in the 1960s) result from groupthink.

Q: **Does conformity play any role in jury decisions (22)?**

A: Absolutely. Recall the study by Solomon Asch. Subjects were asked to judge the length of line segments and had to decide to go with their own true beliefs or to side with the group (who gave the wrong answer). On about one-third of the trials, subjects went along with the group. In this situation, the "evidence" was quite clear. Subjects are not confused or unsure of the right answer. Nonetheless they go along with the group. As the evidence becomes more ambiguous, the conformity effect will become more pronounced. In a jury trial, it is likely that the evidence is not as clear-cut as in the Asch situation. Supporting this position, many authors have noted that the best predictor of a jury outcome is the initial vote taken by the members before deliberation.

Q: **Does group size affect the quality of decision making? If smaller groups make better decisions, why do we have juries composed of 12 people (23)?**

A: There are many factors that influence the quality of group decision making, e.g., the status structure in the group, the degree of cohesiveness (the "we feeling"), and the extent to which group members accept a common goal. In general, the quality of group decisions is inversely related to group size— smaller groups tend to make "better" decisions than larger groups. It is difficult to give an exact "cutoff" point, but groups of 3 or 4 probably make better decisions than groups of 12. So why the jury of 12?

The notion of a 12-person advisory group for justice dates back to medieval times. A millennium ago, all legal decisions were made by the king or queen of the day. Henry II of England set up an "advisory group" around 1166 A.D. to keep him informed of any transgressions against the state. This group was to be composed of 12 men for every 100 men in the area. In reality, this was a group of spies and informers rather than a group of impartial peers. Nonetheless, the notion of 12 to advise on legal decisions was maintained when a more formal justice system was introduced centuries later. Not all states use a jury of 12 peers. In some cases, the jury is composed of 6 people rather than 12. The data indicate that decisions reached by 6-person juries are as "good" as, if not better than those reached by a 12-person jury.

Q: **Are some of the activities seen in Frosh Week based at least partly on deindividuation (24)?**

A: Absolutely. Recall that deindividuation is the tendency to engage in wild, impulsive behavior brought about by a heightened lack of self-awareness. This could be the result of an external focus, high levels of arousal, high group cohesion, or practically any variable that reduces your psychological sense of self. In the classic study by Phil Zimbardo, subjects were brought to the lab and given lab coats and hoods to wear while they recommended levels of electric shock for another individual who made many errors on a memory test. Compared to the individuated group (own clothes, name tags), the deindividuated subjects gave higher shock settings. Dressing in a common uniform, particularly one that masks your identity, will generate a certain amount of deindividuation. Once in this state, you have lowered concerns about being evaluated and lessened your ability to monitor your own behavior.

Q: **What is the "small world" effect (25)?**

A: Stanley Milgram was not only interested in obedience to authority, but was also intrigued by many real-world problems dealing with social networks. He termed one of these problems, the "small world" problem. The notion is simple. If I showed you a picture of a randomly selected person you did not know, how many people would you have to ask until you found someone who knew the target individual?

Milgram prepared a file with background information on a particular target person and showed the file to a subject. If the subject knew the target person (by his or her first name), the study was over and the chain ended. However, if the subject did not know the target, the subject was to pass the file along to a friend—a person they knew by first name and whom they expected might know the target person.

Now think about this for a minute. How many passes do you think would be necessary to identify any particular target? Milgram found that the median number of passes was 5, with a range of 2 to 10 people. He concluded that it is, indeed, a small world after all.

For more information, see the article by Milgram in *Psychology Today*, May, 1967, p. 60–67.

Abnormal Psychology: Disorders and Treatment

Long before a consideration of neurons, sensory receptors, and cognitive dissonance, the idea of diagnosing and treating mental disorders defined psychology for many students. This is what you signed up to hear about in your psychology course. I hope by now you've realized that psychology is an incredibly diverse field of study encompassing many areas of scientific inquiry. As I suggested in an earlier chapter, we must understand "normal" behavior in order to comprehend the "abnormal". **NOTE:** The answers given below address issues at the level of introductory psychology. Whenever you have a concern about your health (mental or physical), you should consult a qualified health care professional.

Q: I've heard people use the term "crackpot" for someone who was mentally ill. Where does this term come from (1)?

A: Good question. Apparently the term dates back to 19th century England and describes a condition that affected the lower class, working poor. It was common at the time to use a ceramic tea pot with a lead core to brew tea. This in itself was not a problem. But if the ceramic outer layer cracked, it would expose the lead core and the tea would be infused with traces of lead. Lead is toxic and will result in brain damage.

This happened often with the tea pots, and the poor were unable to afford new ones. Thus, the lower classes were more likely to be "crackpots".

Q: **Is there any relationship between phases of the moon and mental disorders (2)?**

A: It has long been believed that the lunar cycle can influence the onset of mental disorders. For example, consider the term "lunatic" or "lunacy"— both imply some relation to the moon. Many people feel that the full moon somehow brings on a rash of mental problems and the folklore surrounding the legend of a "werewolf" may stem directly from this belief. Anecdotally, there have been reports of increased patient demand at mental health facilities during, or shortly after, a full moon. So, is there any evidence for some kind of relationship?

The data indicate quite strongly that there is no relationship whatsoever. This holds across a number of very different dependent variables, e.g., calls to a crisis center in Vancouver (Bickis, Kelly, & Byrnes, 1996), behavioral reports of patients in a long-term care facility (Vance, 1996), admissions to psychiatric hospitals in Switzerland (Sheidegger & Degonda, 1997), reported suicides (Gutierrez-Garcia & Tusell, 1997), or penalties in hockey games (Russell & Dua, 1985). In all cases, there was absolutely no relationship between the incidence of the behavior in question and phase of the moon.

So why do we continue to believe in this relationship? An interesting possibility is suggested by Raison et al. (1999). They argue that there may have been a relation before the invention of modern lighting. In these earlier times, the full moon would have been a significant source of light at night, sufficient to disrupt sleep cycles. Such disruption would likely have been sufficient to induce periods of mania in those suffering from bipolar disorder or to cause seizures in those with epilepsy. Modern lighting has "masked" the effect, particularly in urban areas. For more information on this topic, see the article by Raison et al. (1999).

Raison, C., Klein, H., & Steckler, M. (1999). The moon and madness reconsidered. *Journal of Affective Disorders, 53(1)*, 99 –106.

Q: **What is "normal" anyway? If reality is based on perception, how can we label a schizophrenic as "abnormal" (3)?**

A: We use the terms "normal" and "abnormal" quite frequently when discussing mental disorders. Implicit in this terminology is the idea that we can somehow define how a "normal" person functions, thinks, behaves, etc. You correctly point out that psychological reality is based to a large extent on our perceptions. In addition, this process is influenced by culture and environment.

Consider something as straight-forward as visual perception. In the industrialized world, the phenomenon of constancy scaling is part of depth perception. Once we locate an object in space we psychologically adjust the size of the object as indicated by the depth cues. Thus, we realize that a 747 is really a large object when it is flying overhead even though the retinal image is very small.

This phenomenon gives rise to various visual illusions such as the Müller-Lyer or arrowhead illusion (see diagram). The two lines really are equal in length, but they don't look that way. The one with the open arrow heads looks longer.

Gibson has suggested that size constancy scaling is, in part, a consequence of living in a rectangular environment. In the industrialized world, we are exposed to edges, corners, and rectangular structures all the time. But this is not the case in other cultures. For example, tribes on the plains of Africa do not build rectangular houses. They live in semi-circular structures. Furthermore, there are few depth cues available. If you were to show one of these individuals the arrowhead illusion, they would correctly indicate that the two lines are exactly the same length. So, are these people somehow "abnormal"?

Not at all. The concept of normal must be referenced to the experience of people in the culture. Most do not show size constancy scaling, thus, this becomes our standard for "normal" visual perception on the plains of Africa. In a similar fashion, we can refer to normal cognitive function in Western society. If most people do not hear voices when nobody is communicating to them, this becomes our standard against which to judge abnormal behavior. Note that the concept of "normal" is really a statistical definition -- it is referenced to the behavior of most people. You should also remember that "abnormal" behavior must pose a problem to the individual before we would consider it a part of a clinical disorder.

Q: **What's the difference between a psychologist and a psychiatrist (4)?**

A: A psychiatrist is a medical doctor. He or she will have an M.D. degree, will have been trained in general medicinal practice, and will have spent a number of years specializing in various therapies. Only a psychiatrist can prescribe drugs for the treatment of mental disorders. A psychologist will have a degree in clinical psychology. A Ph.D. psychologist will have been trained in research techniques and various clinical therapies. A psychologist with a Psy.D. degree typically will have more clinical and less research training. The amount of training for a Ph.D. or a Psy.D. will vary from place to place, but typically, you're looking at 4 or 5 years in graduate school. Please note that someone claiming to be a therapist will not necessarily have a graduate degree in either medicine or psychology. In most states and provinces, you can call yourself a therapist or a counselor without certification. However, the terms "psychiatrist" and "psychologist" are protected -- one must be licensed by an appropriate agency and it is illegal to use the term without certification. If you are seeking psychological services, it is a good idea to request a referral from your family doctor, phone a local professional association, or look in the yellow pages under "psychiatrists" or "psychologists".

Q: **Who do psychologists see for help (5)?**

A: Other psychologists, of course! Whenever someone has a mental problem, it is most appropriate to talk to a mental health professional, and this applies to psychologists themselves. First of all, not all psychologists are trained to deal with clinical problems; you need to talk to an individual who has the appropriate training in order to deal with the difficulty. It would be unwise also to "treat yourself" for a serious mental disorder even if you were appropriately trained—you may be less than objective in your analysis.

Note: Freud thought it important for the analyst to

undergo psychoanalysis him- or-herself in order to get in touch with his or her own unconscious processes. Freud gained much insight into his own theories through this procedure.

Q: **What is an "anxiety attack" (6)?**

A: Many people feel anxious about something from time to time. Will I get to work on time? What if I say something wrong while I'm out on a date with ___? Can I finish the exam on time?
It is perfectly normal to feel anxious in these situations, but we deal with this feeling and, hopefully, get on with things. Anxiety becomes a clinical problem when you can no longer deal with it. There are several disabling clinical disorders referred to as Anxiety Disorders. These include Generalized Anxiety Disorder, Phobic Disorder, and Obsessive-Compulsive Disorder. Psychologists refer to crippling anxiety attacks as panic attacks. Individuals experiencing panic find themselves in a state of acute terror with a high level of arousal. They experience increased heart rate, dizziness, and shortness of breath. These symptoms may last for several minutes. Perhaps most troubling is that the individual cannot identify what triggered the attack, so shortly after it finally ends, they can't help but worry about when the next one might begin! The typical treatment involves tranquilizers such as Valium.

Q: **I have a history of bipolar disorder in my family. How can I tell the difference between everyday mood swings and real disorder (7)?**

A: Bipolar disorder is a mood disorder characterized by alternating periods of depression and mania. The switching cycle may be fast or slow, and is not necessarily triggered by external circumstances. If members of your immediate family (parents, siblings, or offspring) have a mood disorder, you yourself are 10 times more likely to develop a similar problem. For bipolar disorder, the concordance rate for identical twins is 72% (if one twin has the disorder, the other twin has a 72% chance of getting the disorder too). So, if there is a history of bipolar disorder in your family, you are at risk. The big difference between everyday mood swings and a clinical disorder is in the severity of the symptoms and the length of time they are experienced. For example, we all get "depressed" from time to time, but if this depression lasts for more than two weeks and you have extremely negative thoughts (thoughts of suicide, for example), then you might be considered clinically depressed. If you have any concerns about your mood swings, please talk to your family physician or consult a psychologist. They can help you sort this out.

Q: **I've heard that depression is not a thought disorder. However, if a depressed person considers suicide, isn't that an example of a thought disorder (8)?**

A: When we use a diagnostic system such as DSM-IV, we classify disorders according to their primary symptoms—what most distinguishes one disorder from another. Depression is classified as a mood disorder, indicating that the primary disruption involves how a person feels rather than how they think. Depressed individuals feel worthless and useless. They may also feel that they are a burden to their family, friends, and society. Furthermore, they believe that they cannot do anything about their situation. Severe cases of depression may include symptoms such as hallucinations and delusions (classic examples of disorganized thought), but this is rare. If depressed individuals think about suicide, they consider it a "rational" solution to their problems. Yes, such thoughts are not "normal," but they do not reflect the disorganized thought pattern seen in other disorders such as schizophrenia.

Q: **What is the underlying cause of a phobia (9)?**

A: A phobia is an irrational fear of some object, category or event. The fear experienced is intense, so much so that the individual is often incapable of leaving their own home lest they encounter the feared object. Phobias may be quite specific (e.g., fear of snakes) or more general and social in nature (e.g., fear of being seen by others). There are more than 200 recognized phobias, but all would be classified as anxiety disorders according to DSM-IV. Please note that most of us experience such fear from time to time, but this fear becomes a clinical issue when it interferes with the individual's life.

The underlying cause of a phobia depends for the most part on the perspective or approach you take with respect to mental disorders. For example, from the psychodynamic perspective, the existence of a phobia would suggest that the individual has some deep-rooted, unconscious problem that has been repressed. The behavioral perspective would argue for the role of classically conditioned emotional responses. The target object is a conditioned stimulus that has been paired with an unconditioned stimulus in the past, and the fear is a conditioned response. The exact cause is difficult to pin down, but a behavioral therapy (e.g., exposure) seems to be a fairly effective treatment in cases where the phobia has a specific target.

Q: **What is it called if you are afraid of sex (10)?**

A: This is a difficult question to answer without knowing more details. Nonetheless, there are a few possibilities. Hypoactive sexual desire is a disorder in which "sexual fantasies and desire for sexual activity are persistently or recurrently diminished or absent, causing marked distress or interpersonal difficulties" (DSM-IV, 1994). This is a fairly frequent problem affecting 20% of women and 10% of men. It may be very general or specific to one person or situation and it may be caused by a number of factors including boredom or unhappiness in a relationship, depression, or substance abuse. Generally, in hypoactive sexual desire disorder, testosterone levels are abnormally low and drugs may be prescribed to remedy the situation.

Sexual aversion disorder is a more serious variation. It involves "persistent or recurrent aversion to and avoidance of almost all genital sexual contact with a sexual partner, causing marked distress and/or interpersonal difficulties" (DSM-IV, 1994). Like hypoactive sexual desire, sexual aversion disorder may be general or specific to one person or situation and occurs more often in women. Sexual trauma (e.g., rape, and abuse) is often involved. Treatment would include some kind of talk therapy, often combined with an antidepressant or anti-anxiety drug.

If an individual is diagnosed with a phobic disorder, the term used would be sexophobia (or heterophobia). Phobic disorders are classified as anxiety disorders and the treatment would likely include behavioral (or cognitive) therapy, and an antianxiety medication.

Q: **What is Tourette's Syndrome (11)?**

A: Tourette's Syndrome is a rare disorder
       characterized by involuntary body movements and
       vocal outbursts, which are sometimes obscene
       (although the use of profanity occurs in only about
       30 percent of the cases). Onset is early in
       childhood (in almost all cases, before the age of
       18), and the condition may worsen as the individual
       grows older. Incidence is higher in males than
       females. The cause is mostly unknown, but there
       seems to be a strong genetic link. Metabolism of
       the neurotransmitters dopamine and serotonin is
       abnormal. A common treatment is mild sedation
       with tranquilizers.

Q: **Does serotonin have an effect on depression?
       Can it induce self-harm (12)?**

A: One of the major theories of depression is the
       Monoamine Hypothesis. This theory suggests that
       the problem in cases of major depression is an
       abnormal level of one or more of the monoamines--
       norepinephrine, dopamine and serotonin.   Support
       for this theory comes from the observation that
       effective antidepressant drugs (such as tricyclics
       and MAO inhibitors) will increase the level of these
       neurotransmitters, relieving the symptoms of
       depression.

       Newer antidepressants such as Prozac or Zoloft
       target only serotinin. They block the re-uptake of
       serotonin, effectively increasing the amount
       available in the synapse. Because of this action,
       they are referred to as Selective Serotonin
       ReUptake Inhibitors (SSRI's). The SSRI's seem to
       be more effective in the treatment of depression
       than either the tricyclics or MAO Inhibitors.
       Perhaps this is because depressed patients

consistently show a chronically low level of serotonin, while levels for the other monoamines tend to vary.

Can serotonin induce self-harm? I am not aware of any data indicating that this may be an effect of increased serotonin levels resulting from the treatment of depression.

Q: **What was wrong with Jack Nicholson in the movie, "As Good as It Gets" (13)?**

A: In this film, Nicholson plays Melvin Udall, a bigoted New York writer who has to come to grips with his friends, relationships and life. Nicholson has a number of problems, but appears to suffer from obsessive-compulsive disorder (OCD). OCD is an anxiety disorder characterized by repeated, unwanted thoughts (the obsession) and repetitive behaviors performed in the belief that they will reduce the thoughts (the compulsion). Common obsessions include self-doubt, fear of performing a prohibited act in public, concern with dirt, germs, etc. Compulsions typically involve rituals of counting, checking or cleaning. For example, an individual might believe that she is picking up germs from everything she touches in the house. In order to reduce her distress, she might engage in a washing ritual where she must wash her hands 500 times each morning, afternoon and evening. This could be followed by a face wash (200 times in the clockwise direction, and 200 times counterclockwise). Such behavior will eventually result in damage to the skin, and it is typically at this point that the individual seeks help. Nicholson had similar washing rituals in the movie.

Q: Is there such a thing as borderline personality disorder (14)?

A: Personality disorders are a little more difficult to understand as compared to the classic mental disorders such as depression and schizophrenia. A personality disorder basically means that an individual displays behavior that is more troubling for the people around them than it is for themselves. For example, antisocial personality disorder involves a lack of concern for the rights of others, violation of other's rights, the inability to form friendships, and often, illegal activity such as robbery and even murder. There are many categories of personality disorder (schizoid, paranoid, narcissistic, etc), each reasonably well-defined by a specific set of symptoms.

Borderline personality disorder, by contrast, is a very broad and ill-defined category. There seems to be an instability in mood and relationships. Individuals with this disorder do not have a clearly defined self-image and may draw heavily on others for such an image. Consequently, they do not like to be alone, may feel betrayed by others, and can reject a friend over the most trivial of problems. Other symptoms include poor anger control, recklessness, and possibly, self-abuse.

I should note that there is a good deal of controversy over this classification. Many feel that it is not a specific personality disorder at all. They point out that individuals suffering from "borderline personality disorder" often have experienced physical and/or sexual abuse. Thus, we are really looking at a stress-related disorder. Regardless of the label, this is a disorder that deserves attention.

Q: **In Dissociative Identity Disorder is it possible for one personality to be "blind" while the others have normal vision (15)?**

A: Indeed it is. In Dissociative Identity Disorder (formerly known as Multiple Personality Disorder) one personality may be effectively blind while the other has 20/20 vision. One personality may wear glasses while the other does not. This seems very strange to us, but there have been many reports of individuals adopting extreme shifts in both behavior and psychological functioning when "switching". For example, in the classic case of Sarah and Maud, Sarah was a conservative, proper woman with an above average I.Q. Her alter, Maud, was brash, promiscuous, and had a tested I.Q. about 6 standard deviations lower. And she smoked as well! It is important to remember that Dissociative Identity Disorder is not really about having multiple personalities. Rather, it reflects unconnected "chunks" of psychological and behavior patterns— pieces of identity that an individual has fashioned to deal with the real world. Since the cause of the disorder typically is extreme childhood abuse, it may well be that the best way to cope is to "pretend" that you are someone completely opposite to who you really are.

Q: **Can psychological blindness correct itself (16)?**

A: Definitely. Remember that the problem in this case is psychological. There is nothing wrong with the visual system either at the level of the retina or in the visual cortex. Everything "works," but the patient cannot see. Freud suggested that this kind of problem was a conversion reaction to some kind of trauma. For example, an individual may have witnessed a horrible accident, and feeling guilty, they have repressed the memory by psychologically refusing to see anything. Some kind of talking therapy would be recommended to help the individual deal with the trauma and the feeling of guilt. Once the problem is addressed, the blindness will vanish.

Q: **Can you become addicted to the Internet (17)?**

A: Absolutely! From a psychological perspective, you can become "addicted" to almost anything from drugs to gambling to running. Most people will report feeling a "high" or a "rush" when engaging in an addictive behavior. This results in a very clear-cut learning situation, where you are rewarded for a particular behavior and, thus, the behavior increases in frequency. Addictions are not limited to drugs or situations that produce some kind of physiological dependency. Classic physiological addiction would include tolerance (you become used to a particular level and need more and more to get the high) and withdrawal (you experience anxious, negative feelings when the behavior stops or the drug wears off) effects. However, these symptoms do not always appear, even in drug addiction. Thus, many people believe that the psychological effects are the more powerful.

Surfing the net can produce the same kind of feelings. People can become so captivated that they lose track of time and in extreme cases, may report pain in their fingers and wrists from overuse of the mouse and keyboard! It is estimated that about 6% of Internet users are, in fact, addicted.

Q: How many years following a traumatic experience can a person be affected by post-traumatic stress syndrome (18)?

A: This is a difficult question to answer because the severity and time course (how long it lasts) of this disorder depend on many factors. There are reports of Vietnam War veterans who still experience Post-traumatic Stress disorder (PTSD) today, over 20 years after the events took place. PTSD is an anxiety disorder according to the DSM-IV classification. Anxiety disorders involve intense feelings of fear or anxiety for prolonged periods of time. Included in this category are panic attacks, phobias, and obsessive-compulsive disorder. With PTSD, the individual has been exposed to an extremely frightening or disturbing event (a traumatic experience) and tends to relive or re-experience the event long after it is over. Obviously, this keeps the anxiety level high and in addition to the fear, the individual will tend to avoid those stimuli that remind her/him of the trauma. Research indicates (e.g., Card, 1987; Vernberg et al., 1996) that having a positive coping strategy -- one that allows you to make sense of the event-- is an important factor in dealing with the trauma. A good social support system also is valuable.

Q: How do you treat an anxiety disorder (19)?

A: To a certain extent, it depends on the kind of anxiety disorder we're talking about. For example, a phobic disorder may be approached with a behavioral treatment such as systematic desensitization. An individual with panic disorder may benefit from biofeedback and relaxation training. An obsessive-compulsive disorder may require further intervention. Since the basis of these disorders is anxiety, a common element in the treatment may be some kind of relaxation training. Drug treatments will vary as well. In general, an antianxiety drug is prescribed such as a benzodiazepine (a common one is diazepam— valium). This seems most effective for generalized anxiety disorder. An individual with obsessive-compulsive disorder will typically respond better to an antidepressant such as Prozac.

Q: **In treating obsessive-compulsive disorder, why is Prozac (a seratonin reuptake inhibitor antidepressant) given (20)?**

A: It would seem that a person suffering from an anxiety disorder would want to avoid an antidepressant medication. You make a good observation here. Why would we treat obsessive-compulsive disorder (an anxiety disorder) with an antidepressant like Prozac?

The key lies in the action of the drug itself. As you indicate, Prozac inhibits the re-uptake of serotonin. Thus, for a person taking Prozac, the action of serotonin in any synapse is prolonged since the re-uptake process is inhibited. Since Prozac is quite effective for obsessive-compulsive disorder, this would lead us to believe that one cause is decreased activity of serotonin (not enough released, ineffective binding sites, etc.). Many researchers believe that the serotonin pathways are involved in the inhibition of species-specific behaviors. Thus, we show the compulsion because we have an inadequate neurological system to inhibit such behavior. But why is Prozac effective for depression?

Recall that a major theory of depression is the monoamine hypothesis--people with unipolar depression show decreased activity of these neurotransmitters. Typically, we look at dopamine, but serotonin also is a monoamine.

Q: **Is electroconvulsive therapy (ECT) always beneficial (21)?**

A: No. Sometimes ECT has little or no effect and may result in the patient getting worse. There can be damage to the cortex as well. Modern ECT attempts to minimize the danger by giving the patient a muscle relaxant (so that the convulsion generated by ECT does not break bones) and a general anaesthetic (when ECT was first introduced, the patient remained awake for the procedure). In addition, the patient must consent to the procedure. The number of treatments in a therapy series ranges between 3 and 12, and the shock is delivered only to the right hemisphere to prevent a loss of verbal memory. We are not completely sure how ECT works, but many think it achieves the desired effect by disrupting REM sleep. Please note: ECT is a treatment of last resort offered only to those who can consent and are in serious danger of suicide. It is used only in a small fraction of cases.

Q: **Is it common to mix treatments for various disorders, for example, electroconvulsive therapy (ECT) and lithium (22)?**

A: Therapy is rarely unidimensional. For example, in the treatment of a specific problem, a psychiatrist will often use a combination of drugs and talking therapy to control and resolve different aspects of the disorder. Occasionally, it may be necessary to take multiple drugs during treatment, or two seemingly different approaches. The treatment of choice for Bipolar Disorder is lithium. This drug is prescribed to control the manic phase of the disorder and is effective in approximately 80 percent of the cases. Typically, the control of the mania results in an associated decrease in depressive symptoms as well. But this does not always happen. It may be necessary to treat the depression independently. If an antidepressant drug (for example, Prozac) is not successful, the psychiatrist might try another drug (for example, a tricyclic). ECT is a treatment of last resort for severe depression and would be administered only if all other treatments had failed, the patient was suicidal, and the patient could consent to the treatment.

Q: **Is lithium the only drug treatment for bipolar disorder (23)?**

A: Bipolar disorder is one of the two major types of mood disorders. A bipolar patient will cycle from the depths of depression to the unbounded elation of mania where anything seems possible. One must be very careful when treating bipolar disorder. Standard antidepressants may actually make the situation worse and drive the patient into "rapid cycling." The drug treatment of choice for bipolar disorder has been lithium carbonate, marketed under a number of brand names, such as Eskalith. To date, we're not completely sure how lithium works, but it seems to influence sodium transport during synaptic communication. In addition, it facilitates the uptake of both norepinephrine and serotonin, thus reducing the availability of these neurotransmitters in the synapse.

While lithium is the drug of choice, it is not the only option. When lithium is not effective, the physician may turn to divalproex sodium, an anticonvulsant commonly known as Depakote or Epival. This seems to stabilize mood, primarily by increasing the levels of GABA in the brain. An additional drug, such as Lorazepam, may be given to assist in stabilizing the patient's mood. If all drug treatments are ineffective, the recommendation may be to administer electroconvulsive shock therapy (ECT). This course would only be pursued in severe cases and with the patient's consent. As always, drug therapy is often more effective if some form of "talk" therapy is used as well.

Q: **I've heard that Prozac has few, if any side-effects. Is this true (24)?**

A: Prozac (the trade name for fluoxetine hydrochloride) has been presented by some as the miracle treatment for depression. It is true that Prozac seems more effective and has fewer side-effects than other treatments (for example, an MAO inhibitor). But all drug treatments have side-effects, some more serious than others, and some only in interaction with other drugs. A few of the common side-effects of Prozac include: nervousness, insomnia, headache, and increased sweating. Patients may notice a disruption in REM sleep. Less frequently reported side-effects include: dizziness, flushing, tremors, decreased heart rate, ringing in the ears, nausea, vomiting, dry mouth, abdominal pain, itching, sore muscles, and swelling. Prozac works by blocking the reuptake of serotonin. In essence, serotonin remains in the synaptic gap for a longer time interval and this seems to have a mood-enhancing effect.

Q: The father of a friend of mine has recently gone on Prozac to treat his depression. He has become short-tempered (he was previously very mild mannered) as well as having short-term memory problems. He seems to be forgetting many important events of late (such as colleges she has applied to, etc.) and even major events from the past (five or six years ago) such as family vacations. Could Prozac cause these changes in behavior, or are the changes more likely due to other circumstances or illness (25)?

A: The symptoms you describe are not typical side-effects of Prozac (see the previous question). However, one cannot always be certain of the effects of any drug in a particular individual situation—there may be other drugs interacting with the Prozac, or even individual differences in tolerance. Your friend's father should consult his family doctor in this case to make sure that there is no adverse drug effect taking place. The memory loss you describe should be addressed as well.

Q: What is Gestalt Therapy (26)?

A: Gestalt therapy is a humanistic approach to psychotherapy. The aim of Gestalt therapy is to help people become more in touch with their feelings. Developed by Fritz Perls, Gestalt therapy focuses on the here and now and encourages people to be responsible for their feelings and behavior. To help individuals get in touch with their feelings, Gestaltists use a variety of role-playing exercises. Communication is very important and the therapist relies on both verbal and nonverbal feedback. The Gestalt approach is sometimes criticized for being self-centered and somewhat callous. The therapist demands brutal honesty in all interactions and encourages individuals to concentrate on their own needs and desires, sometimes at the expense of others' needs.

You may be surprised to learn that it was Fritz Perls who said: " I do my thing, and you do your thing. I am not in this world to live up to your expectations, and you are not in this world to live up to mine. You are you and I am I. And if by chance we find each other, it's beautiful. If not, it can't be helped."

Q: **What is St. John's Wart (27)?**

A: St. John's Wart is an herbal remedy derived from the Hypericum plant family. The remedy has not been approved for use by the FDA, but is regulated in several European countries. Applied externally, it is used to treat wounds and bruises. Taken internally, it is touted as an antidepressant. The pharmacological action is not fully understood. Some claim that the action is much the same as with fluoxetine (Prozac), but whether or not St. John's Wart blocks the reuptake of serotonin is debatable. Several double-blind studies indicate that the remedy is effective for the treatment of depression-there are fewer relapses in patients given St. John's Wart compared to a control group. If this herbal remedy should prove to be clinically useful and meets the FDA standards, you might find that it will become a leading treatment for depression. Supporters claim that it has fewer side-effects than standard antidepressant medication, and patients do not report any sexual dysfunction. More research is needed, however, to fully validate these claims.

Q: **Without any consideration of the FDA, in your opinion, does St. John's Wort work? Are there conditions and dosages to determine its effects (28)?**

A: Regarding St. John's Wort, the jury is still out. This herbal remedy has been used in many parts of Europe and some double blind tests indicate that it is effective. The action is similar to Prozac, i.e., it appears to be a selective serotonin reuptake inhibitor. However, it is probably too early to a definitive judgement of "safe"—we need more research.

NOTES

NOTES

NOTES

NOTES

NOTES

NOTES

NOTES

NOTES

NOTES

NOTES

NOTES

NOTES

NOTES

NOTES